Barrow-in-Furness
remembered

The Lighthouse helter-skelter ride draws the crowds in 1907.

BARROW-IN-FURNESS
remembered

BILL MYERS

First published 2000
Copyright © Bill Myers, 2000

Reprinted in 2008 by
The History Press
The Mill, Brimscombe Port,
Stroud, Gloucestershire, GL5 2QG
www.thehistorypress.co.uk

ISBN 978 0 7524 2083 7

Printed and bound in England.

Cover illustration: *Visits to Barrow by fairgrounds brought out huge crowds, as this postcard from around 1910 clearly illustrates.*

It is hard to imagine a scene like this being repeated in Barrow today. A pair of prize beasts behave impeccably outside the butcher's shop at 174 Dalton Road around 1900.

Contents

Introduction		6
1.	Early Days	9
2.	Industries	24
3.	Ships and Submarines	39
4.	Sport and Leisure	54
5.	The Great War	71
6.	Recession Bites	85
7.	Transport	98
8.	Town Life	112

Introduction

Today there is nothing unusual in saying you were born in Barrow; a century ago you would have still been in a small minority. The families who built Barrow, who worked for its fledgling industries and helped it grow from a farming village to a major industrial town were almost all immigrants. They came from rural Lancashire, from Ireland, from Scotland and even from the mines of Cornwall. The boom town of the mid-Victorian era was a melting pot of people, who all brought their distinctive qualities, their customs, sports and forms of religion.

That they came at all was down to one thing, the commercial exploitation of iron from pits which proliferated around Barrow's boundary. One find alone eventually gave up 15,000,000 tons of iron ore and provided the impetus for Barrow to produce its own iron and steel products – including the ships and submarines it is famed for today.

The story of Barrow's road to rapid growth might seem a simple one of geographical and geological luck but there were some serious bumps along the way. Barrow had its spells of great prosperity but there were also years of deep trade depression, problems of poor health and of overcrowding. Barrow was a town of big industries and when one of them was hurt the whole town felt the pain.

The following eight chapters contain a mix of historical notes and extracts from Furness-based newspapers. Many of the newspaper extracts were found during extensive research by the author for an exhibition in Barrow's Dock Museum to mark the centenary of the *North West*

The St Andrew's Pipe Band pictured around 1905. For decades they have been a regular sight at parades and public events.

Tourism 1940s-style with wooden changing huts for more modest visitors to the beach at Walney.

Evening Mail in 1998. The author, who is also assistant editor (Production) at the Evening Mail, uncovered far more material than could possibly have gone on show.

The finished book draws on stories from the Mail – mostly under its earlier title of the North-Western Daily Mail – and from a number of other Furness publications. These include the Mail's former sister paper, The Barrow News, and long-vanished titles such as the Barrow Times and Soulby's Ulverston Advertiser. Furness Newspapers, publishers of the North West Evening Mail, has kindly allowed the use of extracts from its archive editions for this project.

Newspaper articles are fascinating to historians. They are filled with interesting facts which are often not to be found elsewhere – but they rarely paint the whole picture. What you get is a snapshot in time, the latest development of a major story on a particular day. And sometimes you need to be alert to the possibility that those facts have been used to further a particular aim as most Victorian newspapers were set up to support a political party or policy. As late as 1906 the North-Western Daily Mail had flown the flag for Labour candidate Charles Duncan in the Barrow general election fight. Duncan won and was carried shoulder high through the town but the Mail's unfortunate reporter was ejected from the Conservative Club.

In 1926 the General Strike saw the paper speak out as an employer, urging the town not to back the national action in support of the coal miners. This time readers ignored the paper and brought most of the town to a standstill. Even the Mail's own printers joined the protest and there were no papers for a fortnight!

Newspapers in more recent years have striven to be non-partisan, reflecting the mood of the town without picking sides. That policy continues to this day as the Evening Mail records the daily events which will help form the raw material for historians in the future.

The pictures in the book are from the author's own collection of close to 10,000 picture postcards and photographs covering the parts of old North Lancashire, Westmorland and Cumberland which became Cumbria in 1974. Two additional pictures were kindly provided by Brian Edge, a Barrovian now living near Crewe. Exact dates and names have been given on captions where they are known but it is a sad fact that families who carefully store pictures for decades seldom take the trouble to leave notes for future generations. If you have a family album showing the people and places of old Barrow please try to jot a line or two on the back in light pencil to explain what is shown. If you leave it to someone else the knowledge might be lost – and Barrow's history will be the poorer for it.

Dalton Road shoppers come to a standstill for the photographer on this 1900 view.

CHAPTER 1
Early Days

Barrow ironmaster Henry Schneider struck rich in 1850.

The Earth Surrenders its Riches

The finding and profitable, large-scale working of iron-ore reserves surrounding Barrow village provided the spark to turn a quiet rural area into a thriving urban community. Iron outcrops or small opencast sites had been worked in a small way for centuries; even the venerable abbots of Furness Abbey had been involved in disputes over mineral rights. But it was the ambitious Victorian prospectors and the availability of the new method of railway transport through Furness from 1846 which allowed spectacular growth to get under way.

A taste of country life in Barrow around 1904. Water butts are still in use to capture rainfall from the roof.

The engine house at North Stank iron ore mines around 1890.

Discovering Red Gold

The mine with the biggest impact on Barrow's growth and prosperity was the Park Mine on part of the Duke of Devonshire's estate. Henry Schneider and his partner James Davis poured money into the search for the distinctive red stain of iron ore wealth with little initial success until they hit rich in 1850 at what became known as the Park sop.

This find was enormous, more than a quarter of a mile across, going down to a depth of more than 700ft below sea level and eventually producing 15 million tons of iron ore. It was this find more than anything else which sparked the growth of Barrow as the most convenient place to ship out the mineral riches exploited by Schneider and his new partner Robert Hannay. The obvious next step was not just to export the ore from Barrow but to turn it into iron and steel close to the site.

Barrow's Mining Village

The Barrow district spawned its own mining community at Roose where rows of cottages sprang up in the 1870s to provide homes for predominantly Cornish miners. They were here to work the Stank iron ore mines opened by the Barrow Haematite Steel Company in 1872. Roose remained Barrow's mining village until the Stank pits fell silent in 1901.

Barrow iron workers shown by a furnace about to be tapped to allow its molten iron to pour into channels and pig beds cut into compacted sand.

Close to 200 houses in two long rows were built – partly to be close to the main mining area of Stank and Yarlside and because workmen's housing was in such short supply in the centre of Barrow. Life was never easy for miners and the Stank and nearby Yarlside Mines were among the most difficult to work in Furness. The miners were working at depths of close to 400ft below sea level and frequently met with inrushes of water and running sand.

Yarlside's mines had shut in 1900, a victim of ever increasing pumping costs to keep the ore workings dry. Like many of the Furness mines, closure seldom marked the end of the story. Conditions of trade change and in 1910 mine captain Thomas Kneebone was sent from Barrow's other iron ore site at Park Mines to oversee fresh attempts to mine at Yarlside.

To save money a level – a walking access tunnel – was reopened to let water drain from the mines into the River Yarl. Again, to save on pumping costs, they exploited ore lying above the waterline – bringing it to the surface up the shafts of No. 1 and No. 2 Pits. The new breed of cost-conscious miners even found a way to make use of the sand which had dogged earlier attempt to get the iron ore out of Yarlside. It made good foundry moulds and a No. 3, or Sand Pit, was dug to get it out. The First World War brought temporary prosperity of the type enjoyed in the early years of mining. Ore was in great demand for the war effort and up to 150 men were at work.

Mining by the Sea Shore

Barrow's other mining area covered the coastal district around Roanhead and Sandscale. Myles Sandys owned the Roanhead mines area and in 1852 gave a lease to C.S. Kennedy to prospect for iron ore. His two sons Charles and Myles carried on the work after their father's death in 1857 and started the mining company of Kennedy Brothers. The search could bring riches but also brought several false dawns. Many pits were sunk in hope and expectation, worked for a few years and then closed as the ore ran out or proved too expensive to work.

The struggle to keep finding workable bodies of ore was finally given up at Roanhead during the depression years. By the end of the 1920s the remaining pits were derelict. The adjoining mine workings at Sandscale came as close to Barrow as the old British Cellophane factory. The Sandscale Mining Company started prospecting the estate from the late 1870s and sank two shafts working the same body of ore as the Kennedy Brothers. Mining in Furness was like that: competing companies working a few fields apart. In 1892 the Sandscale Mines went to the Kennedy Brothers. The last ore was mined in 1905.

When Barrow was Only Fields

Barrow before the iron boom was a very different place. Readers were offered a trip down memory lane to the 1850s when Barrow was mostly fields in the Barrow News *of*

Despite rapid urban and industrial growth, Barrow still had its quieter rural corners, as shown on this postcard of Roose in around 1904.

24 October 1936. The memories of an eighty-six-year-old woman were not special because of her age but because she had been a Barrovian from birth – a rarity in old folk as the growing Barrow had been populated by immigrants drawn from throughout the British Isles. The paper wrote:

Meet Mrs M. Lake of 148 Rawlinson Street, eighty-six years young and probably the oldest Barrovian in town. Mrs Lake was born in Barrow on 23 November 1849, and will thus be eighty-seven years of age next month. She is in possession of all her faculties, except for slight deafness, and has a remarkable memory.

When our reporter called at Mrs Lake's home he found her sitting by the fireside and quite prepared to talk of Barrow in its very early days.

Mrs Lake should know something about the town. She has lived here all her life and she has seen a big industrial centre spring from a very small village by the sea. Her mother also was born in Barrow. Mrs Lake first saw light in one of a batch of old cottages which used to stand in the vicinity of Schneider Square and were demolished to make way for the residence at present occupied by Dr Ware.

Mrs Lake's aunt kept a dame's school and it was there that the few Barrow children received their early education. For part of the time Mrs Lake had to walk to Newbarns to a school on top of the hill – now the site of Prospect Road. Going to school in those days was not as easy as it is now. There were no streets, only lanes and fields and Mrs Lake had to walk all the way.

There was no Dalton Road then; it was all fields and hedges but a start was being made with the building of houses.

The Toffee Maker

Mrs Lake's memories of Barrow in the 1850s took in a slower-paced, more rural way of life.

To one of the few cottages now standing near Fisher Street, Mrs Lake used to take four copper pennies once a week for a pound of sugar from Old Betty Hartley.

Afterwards Mrs Lake lived on the edge of what was called Clay Pit Lane, where there were about four or five houses, all tumbledown. In one of these houses lived an old woman, who made sticks of toffee and gingerbread men and horses with currants for eyes. Mrs Lake used to help to twist the sticks of toffee.

These houses were at the rear of the present Michaelson Road Post Office and there was a brewery owned by a family named Tyson, whose descendants still farm the district.

The Tyson boys came every morning to attend to the brewery and Mrs Lake used to go for a pennyworth of draughts for her grandfather's hens.

The Strand, as it is now known, was the shore of a tidal channel and there were stepping stones across the water when the tide was down. Over these stones Mrs Lake used to go to bring the milk from the farm on Barrow Island.

When Mrs Lake was a child there was a bank on one side of the Strand and high tides used to come over. When she took her father's breakfasts to the old railway station she sometimes had to wade through the water to the other side where there were four houses, and she had to climb fifteen steps to reach them.

Her grandfather was a platelayer on the railway. He came to Barrow from Dalton at the same time as Mr (later Sir) James

Action from the jubilee ploughing and hedging competition held at Rakesmoor, Barrow, in February 1932.

Ramsden, who came from Liverpool as railway engineer.

The Furness Railway engine *Old Coppernob* was brought to Barrow in pieces in an old tug. Mrs Lake's uncle Mr Robert Thexton helped to build it and was the first man to drive the locomotive.

Mrs Lake can remember the laying of the rails along which the engines of the Furness Railway ran. She was present at the opening of St George's church when the children had to walk in procession and were given medals. She was later married at the church.

The first hospital was situated in Albert Street and Mrs Lake's sister was a nurse there. Mr J. Moody made bricks in Mount Pleasant when there were no houses there and the children used to play round the brick kiln. Later Mrs Lake's grandfather and another man built a house on the same site as the brickworks – 39 Mount Pleasant. At that house her sister was born.

Barrow was only a little village then. 'I have watched it grow,' says Mrs Lake. 'There is many a street and place in it now that I don't know'.

The Road to Growth

By the mid-1860s there was activity everywhere you looked in Barrow. A glimpse of what the town was like in the Klondike days of headlong growth is provided in this extract from the 1866 Furness directory published by P Mannex.

The progress that this town has made is truly wonderful. In 1846 when the line of railway from Broughton to Dalton was opened, Barrow was only a small village of about 300 inhabitants; in 1857 it numbered about 2,000; and now in 1865 its population is not far short of 12,000; and it exhibits the appearance and possesses several of the characteristics of a large and important seaport town.

15

A postcard from around 1903 showing how farm buildings were cleared to make room for the new Hawcoat Methodist church.

Thus has the development of the mineral wealth of this El Dorado, as Furness has been not inaptly designated, and the extension of the railway system caused a town to grow up, which may be said to be a combination in appearance of Birkenhead and a gold-finder's city on the edge of the western prairies of America.

With feelings of gratitude it ought to be acknowledged that the fine old harbour of Piel, so readily made available for the purpose of shipment, has also contributed materially to the rapid growth and prosperity of Barrow.

The pier and the quay, originally of wood, is now a substantial stone structure, on which is a network of lines, and steam cranes, to facilitate the transmission of ore and merchandise to the different vessels. Large quantities of timber are imported from Canada, Norway and Sweden.

The passenger station of the Furness Railway, at the east end of the town, the engine house, and the whole range of buildings adjoining the docks, are characterised by neatness, comfort and solidity.

Another passenger station is about to be erected at Hindpool, near the entrance to the new docks. Immense quantities of iron ore are shipped and consumed here annually.

In 1847, the iron ore carried by the railway was 103,768 tons; in 1857, 562,093, of which 406,615 were sent to Barrow for shipment and consumption at the iron works here, the remainder being carried inward by rail. The annual quantity of iron ore consumed here is 270,000 tons; exported 250,000 tons; and sent inland by rail, 230,000 tons. Of copper ore, the annual shipments for this port are about 3,000 tons, and of slate 6,000 tons out of a produce of about 20,000, the residue being sent inward by rail.

Developing the Docks

The 1866 Mannex directory also outlined the work underway to modernise Barrow dock system and to develop the other attractions offered to business and to those looking at Barrow as a place to live and work.

A great work now in progress is the conversion of the channel between the mainland and Barrow Island into a large dock or float of upwards of 100 acres, similar to that at Birkenhead, with a graving dock of 500ft long and 150ft wide.

These docks, when completed, will be capable of receiving vessels drawing 25ft of water. The docks are nearly a mile in length and between 500 and 600ft wide. There are two floating docks and a timber pond of 60 acres. Engineers are Messrs McClean and Stileman; contractors, Messrs Brassey and Field; agent, Mr John Dent.

In the western part of the town, the attention of every stranger is attracted to a series of erections known as the Haematite Iron Works; also to the work of the Haematite Steel Co, lately erected. The former contain eight furnaces, and the latter will soon be on a scale capable of turning out, weekly, 1,000 tons of steel which is manufactured on the Bessemer process.

The steel works cover 25 acres of land and among the articles manufactured are railway tyres, rails, ship plates and shafting of all descriptions; James Ramsden Esq. is the managing director of the company and J.T. Smith Esq. manager of the works.

The town possesses also extensive timber yards, saw mills and brick works, which give

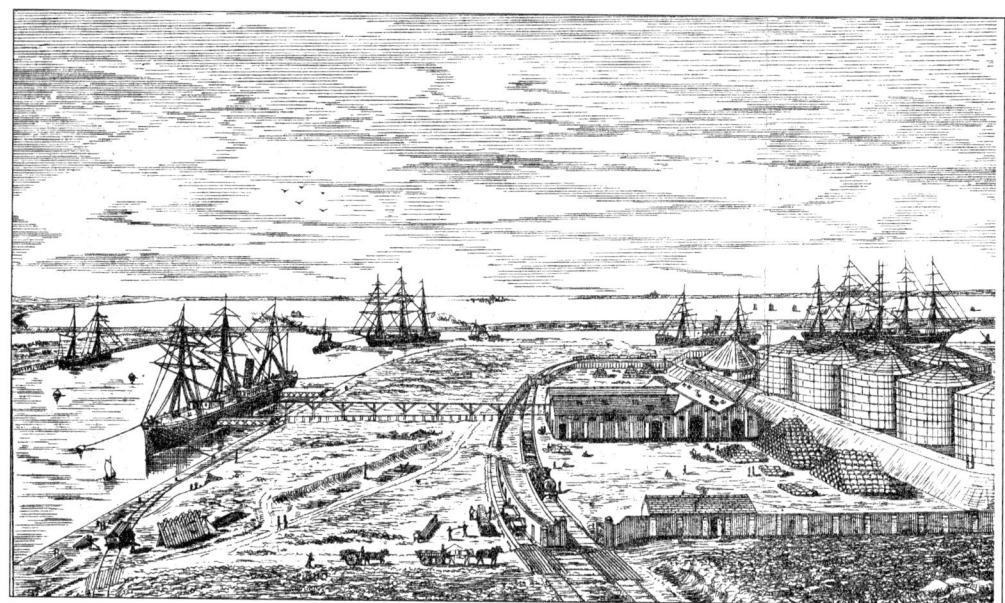

The 1899 storage complex at Barrow docks for petroleum importers and refiners Goodall, Burnip and MacDougall.

employment to a large number of persons; and streets of houses have been speedily produced and are fast filling up the plan of the port of Barrow.

In 1853, the houses, including the remainder of the township of Dalton, were estimated at £60; they are now worth £12,000. Shops have risen in the same period from £60 to £2,600. Cottages are about fourfold what they were in 1853 and inns about twelvefold, while the rateable value of railway property in the district is more than six times what it was in 1853.

Piers, etc. are estimated at more than £3,000 and an item of less than £200, which, except inns, represented the whole industrial enterprise in 1853, has swelled to about £6,000.

The ratio of increase in the township since 1853 is 250 per cent, owing chiefly of course to the rapid progress of Barrow, the new industrial capital of Furness, though Ulverston is still the chief mart for the district and has always been looked upon as the key to the Lakes.

A Fledgling Town's Amenities

The 1866 directory also listed Barrow's small but growing range of social and leisure facilities.

A town hall and covered market, begun in 1864, contains a public room 90ft by 45ft and 30ft in height and will accommodate about 1,000 persons. It is provided with a platform and orchestra and all necessary retiring rooms. The front is ornamental, and contains accommodation for all necessary public offices; a clock tower is also to be added.

The police office is at the south-west corner of the Market Place.

In the town are a Temperance Hall, a thriving Mechanics' Institute, with a good library and news room, on the premises of the railway company; a subscription news room and a Public Library.

Barrow Harbour Hotel, the Bull Hotel, Hartington Hotel, Devonshire Arms Hotel, the Ship Inn, the Hindpool Hotel are all superior buildings and possess every necessary accommodation.

There are several good shops in Barrow, especially those in the Strand. A theatre, erected here in 1864, will accommodate 1,000 persons. Alexander Malcomson, proprietor.

The Barrow Institute, established January 1, 1864, is well supplied with newspapers, periodicals, etc., and the library consists of about 350 volumes. J. Ramsden Esq., president; R. Hannay Jnr Esq., vice-president.

A building society was established in 1863: W. Relph, solicitor and A. Worrall, surveyor. The Lancaster Banking Company

The guide waiting to greet visitors to the ruins of Furness Abbey around 1902. Barrow had history on its doorstep even though it was an industrial new town.

A 1904 view of the Walmsley and Smith Corn Mills seen from the railway tracks.

An Edwardian artist's impression of how the ruins of Furness Abbey would look after a thorough restoration!

has a branch here and a good building is now being erected for their use on the Strand. Messrs Wakefield, Crewdson and Co. of Kendal, have also a branch in this town.

A newspaper, called the *Barrow Herald*, made its first appearance on January 10, 1863. It is well conducted and has already a circulation of about 1,800. Mr James Waddington, publisher and proprietor.

On the coast, about a mile from the town, is the extensive shooting ground of the 37th battalion Lancashire Rifle Corps.

Barrow is well supplied with water and gas. In 1862 gasworks were first established here, by a company under the Limited Liabilities Act; but in 1864 a new Act was obtained by which the works have been transferred to the Furness Gas and Water Company. The apparatus consists of six benches of fire clay retorts, annuller condensers, four screwers eight feet square, dry lime purifiers, station meter and gas holder. The latter is 50ft diameter, 18ft deep and is capable of holding about 36,000cu ft of gas.

Another gas holder now being constructed will be 100ft diameter, 20ft deep, and will be capable of holding 157,000cu ft. The illuminating power is 18 candles and the present number of public lamps is 80.

An abundant supply of water comes from Powka Beck, a distance of nine miles. The principal reservoir extends over 28 acres and is capable of containing 150 million gallons of water. James Ramsden Esq., secretary and Mr John Lewis, manager.

Stone Age Discovery at Barrow

Barrow is very much a Victorian and industrial creation but its roots go back thousands of years. On 18 April 1936 the Barrow News *reported the discovery of an Early Stone Age artefact in Dane Avenue.*

Whilst working on his allotment garden in Dane Avenue, Barrow, on Sunday, Mr Harry Costley, of 6 Dudley Street, Barrow, dug up a finely preserved flint fist hatchet of the Early Stone Age. He found it about 15in deep.

$7\frac{1}{2}$in long by $3\frac{1}{2}$in wide and about $1\frac{1}{4}$in thick in its centre, it is a splendid example of the earliest self-finished type of tool made by man. Professor J.H. Breasted in his *Brief History of Ancient Times* says that the men of the Early Stone Age used the fist hatchet for almost everything. Either end might be used as a cutting edge but it was usually held in the fist by the narrower part and had no handle. It was from 8 to 10in long and sharp enough for man to cut the roots and branches he wanted for food, to shape his fire-making tools and to hew out his heavy wooden club.

These fist hatchets have been found in many places in Europe as well as in other parts of the world.

Bringing the Steam Age to Barrow

Bringing the railway to Barrow took an Act of Parliament – the Furness Railway Act of 1843. It outlined plans for a railway across the Duddon and up the West Cumberland coast.

The steam locomotive Parkside, with crew in front and iron ore wagons behind, in a picture from around 1904.

The railway opened in 1846 with services designed to link Kirkby-Ireleth slate quarries and the Dalton iron ore mines to the shipping jetties on the coast at Rampside. Extensions eventually linked Barrow to Lancaster by 1857, to Coniston by 1859, Lakeside by 1869 and Conishead Priory by 1883. Sir James Ramsden played a leading part in the development of the Furness Railway and was the first locomotive superintendent in 1846.

At first the main line did not pass through the centre of modern Barrow but had a terminal station at St George's Square. When the new Barrow Central Station was built in 1882 the line was extended to the centre of town.

Back in 1848 you could travel first, second or third class. A single ticket from Barrow to Dalton was 1s 6d first class and 6d third class.

The railway was a driving force in the development of Barrow – and not just for its role in moving vast quantities of industrial raw materials. It was also involved in the development of the docks and in the early spate of house-building in the town after finding it difficult to find anywhere locally for its workers to live.

Railway cottages were built in Salthouse Road and in 1854 the Furness Railway Company bought the Hindpool Estate and drew up ambitious development plans.

With financial backing from the Dukes of Devonshire and Buccleuch, James Ramsden, now the railway general manager – and later first Barrow mayor – was able to push ahead with the building project.

The growth of the railway went hand in hand with that of Barrow. It absorbed the Whitehaven and Furness Junction Railway, the Coniston Railway and the Lancaster Railway. The line was opened from Ulverston to Lakeside and branches built to Conishead Priory, Stank, Hawcoat and Stainton.

The Growth of Barrow Docks

As early Barrow grew to export iron ore a series of jetties was built into the channel. The area was covered by the terms of the Barrow Harbour Act of 1848. In 1863 the Furness Railway Company got an Act of Parliament to build docks and expand the harbour. On 19 September 1867 the Duke of Devonshire was able officially to open Devonshire Dock. The procession, opening ceremony and a giant bonfire were watched by a crowd of 25,000.

Devonshire Dock was built to provide a water area of 30 acres, was 2,000ft long and had an entrance width of 60ft and a depth of 22ft. The Graving Dock, now home to the Dock Maritime Museum, was opened in 1872, Buccleuch Dock in 1873 and Ramsden and Cavendish Docks in 1879. Between 1863 and 1879 the Furness Railway spent more than £2 million on the dock system. Barrow was created an independent port on 1 November 1872, although it had had its own Customs House from 1868.

The growing dock system attracted new industries which relied on close links with the sea. The Barrow Corn Mills complex was completed in 1871. Some of the biggest ships of the age kept it supplied with grain from America, Russia and Australia. The Barrow Corn Mills eventually closed around 1967 and the buildings and a bonded warehouse were destroyed by fire.

Another to rely on ships to bring in raw materials was Goodall, Burnip and

Railhead and loading quay at Ramsden Dock, Barrow, in 1907.

Macdougall – importers, refiners and manufacturers of petroleum, lubricating and burning oils. It started in business in 1891 on the site of an old shipyard and held up to 2,500 tons of stocks in huge tanks by the dockside. Crossfield's timber yard and saw mills at Buccleuch Dock imported timber from Canada in 4,500-ton shipments.

Today the Barrow docklands are still active and under the control of Associated British Ports. A major investment saw the opening of the new Ramsden Dock entrance in 1992 on the occasion of the 125th anniversary of the port of Barrow.

CHAPTER 2

Industries

The dramatic event of an ironworks chimney demolition brought out the crowds around 1905.

A Town Built on Iron and Steel

The early part of the nineteenth century saw the village of Barrow established as a small port dealing mainly with the shipment of haematite iron ore. This trade in ore was given a great stimulus by the coming of the Furness Railway in 1846. The railway was able to transport large quantities of ore from mines to port, and Barrow began to expand. Henry Schneider was the most important figure in the local mining industry. He recognized that Furness offered great supplies of haematite ore and limestone, but lacked coal to provide the coke needed to enable iron to be manufactured.

In 1857 the Ulverston and Lancaster Railway was completed, connecting Barrow with the growing railway system. Coke could now be brought in relatively cheaply from Durham and a company was set up by Schneider and a Scot, Robert Hannay, to construct three blast

Few products of Barrow were more unusual than this – a wooden pattern for a Mersey Bar sand pump in 1893.

A new steel bridge arriving by railway at the Walmsley and Smith Barrow Corn Mills on 14 January 1905.

furnaces in Hindpool. The first two started production in 1859.

The experimental work carried out by Henry Bessemer in the 1850s led to a cheap method of producing the previously expensive steel. James Ramsden formed a company to make steel using the Bessemer process and amalgamated with Schneider, Hannay and Company in 1866 to form the Barrow Haematite Iron and Steel Company. Within ten years sixteen blast furnaces were in operation with a capacity to produce 8,000 tons of iron per week.

The line of blast furnaces, each over 60ft high, together with the eighteen 5-ton capacity Bessemer converters, comprised one of the largest iron and steel works in the world. The number of Bessemer converters employed was later reduced by stages to four, which had a weekly production capacity of 7,000 tons of steel.

By 1880 the Siemens open hearth process had been devised. Two 12-ton furnaces were installed. This process did not necessarily require the local haematite ore but could utilize cheaper foreign ore imported through the rapidly developing Barrow dock system. The open hearth process eventually replaced the Bessemer system of steel production at Barrow. The steel produced at Hindpool supplied the rolling mills on the same site. The works was the first in the world to engage in mass production of rails by rolling. Rails became the speciality of the company and were exported in quantity throughout the world.

By the end of the nineteenth century the Barrow Haematite Iron and Steel Company had lost the natural advantages it had once held over competitors. The rapid evolution of technology and approaching obsolescence of plant, together with a gradual slowing of railway construction, made the future uncertain. The First World War temporarily stimulated production, unfettered by much competition, but the inter-war depression made it impossible to modernize the ageing plant sufficiently.

The Second World War provided another boom period which lasted until 1949. This year saw a record production of 5,340 tons of pig iron in a single week. In 1951, the factory was nationalized, and it was sold in 1963 to the Millom Haematite Ore and Iron Company which immediately closed it down with the loss of hundreds of jobs.

The steelworks gained a new lease of life with an experimental arc furnace designed for continuous casting. This was so successful that in 1961 a full-size continuous casting plant was built. The Barco plant was housed in a new, large building in the middle of the old steelworks which was gradually demolished over the years. The steelworks, a tiny remnant of what it had once been, finally closed in 1983 with the loss of 174 jobs. In 1982 the steelworks had lost £350,000.

The demolished site eventually rose again as the Project Furness site, providing a base for factories, car showrooms and the Furness College Channelside Complex.

Looking Closer to Home for Iron

As Spain was torn apart by civil unrest and Europe drifted ever closer to the Second World War, the iron and steel companies of Furness and West Cumbria had to look closer to home for supplies of iron ore. Ironically it was imported ores which helped put many of the Furness mines out of business; now with Spain out of the picture the search for Furness reserves started again. The Barrow News *of 7 November 1936 reported:*

The present trouble in Spain is having its repercussion on the iron and steel industry in this country. The north-west coast is suffering from the inability of certain ironmasters to obtain adequate supplies of foreign ore, and because of that a furnace has been put out of blast at Workington and another has been temporarily damped down. It is hoped the difficulty in obtaining supplies will be overcome and that production in this area will be maintained on the high level which has ruled for many months.

The position at Barrow has not been affected by the shortage of ore supplies from overseas. Some time ago the Barrow Steel Company embarked upon a mining development at Cleator Moor, which has not only provided work for a considerable number of men in one of the most distressed spots in the whole county, but has, especially in the light of current events abroad, proved a most desirable, timely and prudent enterprise.

The tonnage of ore being raised is already substantial and is being augmented week by week. Moreover the metallic content of the ore at Cleator Moor is in the region of 57 per cent, which ranks with the highest grade haematite iron ore in this country. Another important factor is the low phosphoric content of the ore, which enables the company to produce a special low-phosphorus iron for which it has a high reputation.

The Barrow company has further decided

Tapping the furnace at Barrow Ironworks, around 1960.

to re-open the iron ore mines at Yarlside which have been closed for about thirteen years so far as the production of iron ore is concerned, but which have continued producing a high-class foundry sand. This is believed to be the only mined sand in England.

The company is now able to obtain the bulk of its ore requirements from mines in Cumberland and Furness and they also use a certain proportion of Norwegian ore. The reduction of output of pig iron in Cumberland is unfortunate, especially as consumers all over the country are clamouring for supplies. All producers in this area are heavily booked and very little new business is being transacted.

At Barrow production will shortly be increased, work having been completed on the rebuilding of a furnace of greater capacity which will augment the output of semi-special and special haematite pig iron by approximately 1,800 tons per week.

This furnace, it is expected, will come into operation at the end of this year. Moreover, another furnace is being re-lined at the Barrow works, and if circumstances warrant, it will probably be put into operation in the course of another four to five months.

Quotations are not officially changed but with a famine of iron threatening, consumers may be glad to obtain supplies even at a premium. It would appear that there will not be sufficient iron to satisfy all requirements for some time to come.

A considerable proportion of the output at Barrow and Workington is being absorbed in the steel industry, which, in most branches, continues to be exceedingly brisk and makers hold satisfactory order books.

Doom for Ironworks

In June 1962, Millom Ironworks – which had already acquired and shut Askam and Ulverston ironworks – commissioned consulting engineers Campbell, Gifford and Morton of Weybridge, Surrey, to prepare a report on the viability of Barrow Ironworks.

The report showed that Barrow Ironworks had fixed assets worth £1.4 million and was once part of one of the world's biggest integrated iron and steel works. It had been hived off in 1948 in preparation for steel nationalization and by 1962 its furnaces were outdated and its modern ore crushing and sinter plants were working well under capacity. The sinter plant had been built in 1948 by Hunting Herberlein and was capable of producing 10,000 tons per week.

Using the two good furnaces – Nos 3 and 4 – the ironworks could produce 7,000 tons of pig iron per week. No. 2 furnace was in a poor condition with some of its metal plates buckled and bulging. It had already produced 300,000 tons of iron and was not considered to be worth a major re-build.

As of April 1962 there was a stock of 17,000 tons of unsold pig iron; the company was losing money and was only working at 55 per cent of capacity. It had last made a profit in 1960. The Barrow Ironworks had 320 process workers and 250 general and maintenance workers. The report proved fatal for Barrow Ironworks and it was closed in 1963.

Last view of a doomed ironworks: the pig iron dumps at Barrow in 1962.

Abbots Wood, near Furness Abbey, was the palatial home of Barrow's best-known founding father, Sir James Ramsden.

The Evening Mail on 17 January 1963 told readers the writing had been on the wall for Barrow Ironworks for some time.

This shock news for Barrow caused little surprise among iron and steel experts. The general reaction was that, in view of the state of the pig iron market, it was surprising that the closure had not come before.

The town realised the impact hundreds of job losses would have and by March 20 churchmen were calling for work to lessen the hardship of the men affected. In a statement they said:

The future is uncertain: ought we to encourage families to uproot themselves and leave Barrow? We are in a special position to know how such things affect the older families with deep roots and life-long associations.

It is our business to be concerned with politics, because politics are about how men live together. Our interest is, of course, with policies, not political parties.

We condemn as unjust a policy which leads to the closing down of the foundation industry of Barrow without first making proper provision for the care of the workers and their families.

A Finger in Every Pie

Sir James Ramsden, the best known of Barrow's founding fathers, lived in splendour at Abbot's Wood. This stately mansion, bought by Barrow Council in 1961 for Civil Defence use but later demolished, was built without regard to cost and had extensive grounds tended by five gardeners. The mansion, overlooking the ruins of Furness

Abbey, had forty rooms and stood in 19 acres of grounds. Inside it had a distinctly medieval feel in keeping with its abbey setting. It was packed with rich furnishings and china.

By the time the council took it on the house was in poor condition and no use could be found for it. Oddly enough, the site later played host to an anonymous concrete building – designed to be the borough control centre in the event of a nuclear attack during the Cold War years.

Ramsden was most closely associated with the Furness Railway but also played a significant role in property development, Barrow docks, the iron and steel industry and shipbuilding.

Monuments in Brick to Gradwell

One of the principal men who literally helped to build Barrow was the Victorian brickmaker William Gradwell. He didn't just make bricks by the hundreds of thousands but also constructed many of the best known buildings in Barrow.

Among them were the Duke of Edinburgh Hotel, St James's church, Hindpool Congregational church, Holker Street School and the Scotch Flats. William Gradwell started in 1844 at Roose as a wheelwright, joiner and carpenter, working largely for local farms. With the growth of Barrow and the need for building timber and carpentry the Gradwell company prospered. He turned his hand to brickmaking, making use of clay from Hindpool and Salthouse Marsh. It developed in pace with the Barrow building boom and employed upwards of 700 men.

Gradwell also produced telegraph poles and railway sleepers designed to last for years in all weathers, by a process of pumping creosote and oil into the timber under pressure.

Industrial accidents were commonplace and even the death of a workman didn't always attract big headlines. Here the 'cantilever crane disaster' at Vickers is shown on a postcard of January 1913.

Damage caused by the major blaze at Waddington's Foundry in Barrow.

William Gradwell became mayor of Barrow in 1881 but died during his term of office on 6 September 1882.

Fire Failed to End a Business

Engineers and founders Waddington's were perhaps best known for the fire which almost destroyed their premises. The great blaze took place on 21 November 1906 and caused extensive damage. The business, which employed around 150 men, was restored and survived until the recession of the early 1920s. Then it was not fire but a lack of orders which defeated the best efforts of the owners to keep it going. The foundry and engineering works stood in Hindpool Road with the entrance from a short street almost opposite the bottom of Cornwallis Street, leading to Devonshire Dock Transit Shed and the Corn Mills. The foundry had been established in 1860 and in the early days was known as Waddington and Longbothams.

The firm supplied most of the cast iron bollards and other products for the vessels built in the shipyards on Ironworks Road and also carried out smithwork and later provided steam winches and capstans.

It became an extensive industrial site with a moulding shop with four cranes; one was built by Joseph Waddington's and capable of lifting 20 tons. A smaller shop was used largely for making pipes for use in Barrow. There were three large cupolas for melting iron and a brass foundry with two furnaces. There was also a fitting shop and power came from a 12hp engine.

Wheels for the World

The British Griffin Iron and Steel Company was formed in October 1899 to produced chilled iron wheels and other castings using the latest American techniques. It was based on a 7-acre plot off Ainslie Street and close to the Furness Railway line bought from the Barrow Haematite Iron and Steel Company, according to the Barrow News and Mail's industrial survey for 1903. It was described as being:

Fully equipped with all the necessary and most modern plant and machinery, including electric installation for the output of 100 wheels per day, as well as large chilled castings.

The cost of chilled iron wheels was much less than traditional steel-tyred wheels and when used on electric tramways were guaranteed for 30,000 miles in ordinary use. The name of Griffin was known throughout the world.

At the present time wheels made by the British Griffin Company are in use on about 80 per cent of the tramways in the United Kingdom. They are also extensively used in India and Africa. In India alone nearly 15,000 wheels have been sold, and they are running on the Burma Railways, Assam Bengal Railway, HM Nizan's State Railway, Indian State Railways, Barsi Light Railway, Bengal North Western.

The British Griffin Company is now manufacturing over 1,000 pairs of wheels

Workers at the British Griffin Company pose with examples of cast wheels which were sold throughout the world.

and axles for the Burma Railways, which has already 2,500 British Griffin wheels in use.

Like many Barrow firms, it was badly hit by the major industrial downturn which followed the First World War. By 1923 the Griffin company was in the hands of London receiver Harry Peat and was advertised to be sold in one lot on 14 June. It had offices, a pattern store, engine and boiler houses, an axle machine shop, wheel finishing shop and a foundry – together capable of employing 100. Power came from a 135hp Kerr horizontal steam engine linked to a huge dynamo while the smithy had a 10cwt belt-driven power hammer built by Samuel Platt.

Putting the Fizz into Factory Life

The Barrow Herald was keen to tell its readers about new firms and the use of new technology. On 7 April 1891 it sent a reporter for a first-hand look at how a fizzy drinks company operated.

There is much to be seen of interest in a survey even of a mineral water industry, and particularly is this so in a place like that possessed by the Barrow Mineral Water Company.

An inspection of the manufactory shows clearly that it is replete with the most modern appliances used in trade. The company had the satisfaction of celebrating last week its first birthday.

On entering the workshop, amid the din of machinery can be heard the fizzing of lemonade, ginger beer, ginger ale and multitudinous other 'ades' being bottled and prepared for despatch.

The visitor was fascinated by a new system in use to rapidly fill the bottles.

The liquid is passed to the bottling machine, a cleverly devised instrument by Mr J. Chavasse, which certainly transcends all we have seen and is calculated to work a revolution in this particular part of the trade. The machine is a marvel of simplicity, will fill three bottles simultaneously, and will turn out with the greatest of ease from 180 to 200 dozen per hour.

Money from Old Rope

In a shipbuilding town it made sense to have a business devoted to producing the huge ropes needed to keep a vessel secured while in port. Shaw and Lee's steam ropery rose to the challenge and its work was described in the Barrow News Almanack *of 1898.*

This ropery, which is of modern construction, is situate alongside the yard of Vickers, Sons and Company, Old Barrow. New machinery, possessing the best appliances, is at work and a large trade is done in all classes of rope. The advantageous position of this ropery for shipping and other purposes connected to the port of Barrow and elsewhere is fully appreciated and has exercised an important influence upon the development of the business.

Messrs Shaw and Lee have made hawsers of considerable dimensions – some being as much as 15in circumference – for the largest steamers built at Barrow, including the late troopship *Warren Hastings* for the Indian government.

The firm's manufactures include Manilla, Russian and Italian hemp and jute ropes, flax and hemp spun-yarns (round and square), and they have made a speciality of the production of main driving ropes, crane ropes, block ropes, hoist ropes, in Manilla

A sneak preview of the Airship No. 1 *still in its hangar on 11 May 1911.*

and Italian hemp, and round and square flax gaskin of superior quality from specially selected hemp and torch rope.

The Doomed Flight of the Mayfly

In 1909 there was intense building activity at Cavendish Dock to provide Barrow with a place away from prying eyes for the new wonder weapon of the skies – the airship. They were capable of covering vast distances, striking fear into the hearts of enemies and were able to spy on factories and troop movements without opposition.

The *Penny Illustrated Paper* of 30 October 1909 described the activity at Barrow to create the airship shed. Under a picture of part of Cavendish Dock it said: 'Britain's Secret Airship. Site of the new shed in which the secret airship is now being built for the Admiralty. 'It is situated at Cavendish Dock and as there is only a low embankment separating the shed from the sea, the ship will have a clear passage over open water when completed.'

Work progressed on what was officially *Naval Airship No. 1*. It was locally known as the *Mayfly*; perhaps after the short-lived insect or because few thought it capable of taking off. It should have been finished by June 1910 but the experimental nature of the project led to lengthy delays.

The completed airship underwent successful buoyancy and other tests but disaster struck when it was towed from its hangar at 7 a.m. on Sunday 24 September 1911 ready to rise into the sky. Watched by Admiralty officials and 200 Marines, the *Naval Airship No. 1* began to twist in little more than a light breeze and suddenly collapsed into a crumpled heap with a

Airship No. 1 *after the launch disaster which broke it in half in September 1911.*

ruptured gas bag. Fortunately there were no casualties but a project costing £80,000 had to be abandoned without the airship getting off the ground.

The stricken airship drew crowds of people to Cavendish Dock and featured on a range of postcards sold soon after the event in Barrow shops. The *North-Western Daily Mail* the following day said: 'Before anyone had time to realize what was happening, the aft end of the airship shot up in the air and then collapsed, the fabric covering torn to ribbons and the delicate framework crumpled like matchwood.'

It was not the end of airship building at Barrow and rather more success was had with the R80. Work on it started in April 1918 and was not completed until 1920 when it made a maiden flight of 15 miles over the Irish Sea. The airship had a range of up to 4,000 miles and left Barrow for Howden on 24 February 1921. Only one more airship followed it from the giant hangar, this time for the Japanese. The hangar was eventually broken up for scrap.

One Hundred Miles of Elastic

Barrow has always been noted for the rich variety of its manufacturers, even when steel and ships were the dominant force. It is rare to get a detailed account of what it was like to actually work in a factory, but the North-Western Evening Mail *of 16 February 1950 provided an insight into life at an unusual textile mill.*

A hundred miles of elastic come from Barrow each day. [The] newest industry in Barrow and one which is contributing towards filling the dollar gap by the adoption of an export policy to some of the hard currency areas, is that of elastic braid manufacture. Not a very important sounding industry you may say, but, nevertheless, it is vital.

The firm engaged in this manufacture here is Narrow Fabrics Ltd, which occupies the Greengate Mills. The factory was first opened in 1947, with the encouragement of the Board of Trade in order to absorb a part of the surplus female labour in Barrow. The firm was put into touch with the Barrow and District Development Committee, who gave it assistance in finding suitable accommodation.

Although the building is comparatively small, it has all the modern and time-saving machinery and is second to none in respect of its output. When I stepped into the work room, I was greeted by a shrill-pitched roar, created by the numerous braiding machines with their bobbins spinning round and round plaiting various materials together. Young girls I saw who were minding the machines, seemed quite unperturbed by the deafening sound, although the only way I could make myself understood was by visible signs.

I found the process of manufacture not a particularly complicated one. The factory is supplied with its raw material requirements, which include rayon, spun rayon, bleached and un-bleached cotton and various thicknesses of elastics. The yarn arrives in bundle form and is placed on to winding machines which spin the material around bobbins in preparation for slotting on the braiding devices.

Electrically controlled, the braid bobbins revolve around, plaiting the yarn to the elastic and so knitting long strips. The latter are then measured and reeled by another machine and finally made up into boards or cards ready for despatch.

Part of the firm's supply goes to the large London and provincial stores for retail sale, but the bulk is shipped abroad. Countries being supplied with Barrow's elastic braid include: Peru, Holland, Cyprus, Germany,

The massive lathe shop in the marine engine department at Vickers in 1907.

The Barrow Carting Company at Imperial Mews offered furniture removals and carriage hire. It also knew a thing or two about advertising its services judging by this 1906 postcard!

Malta, Rhodesia, Malay States, Denmark, Norway, all parts of Africa, British Guiana, Pakistan, Ceylon, China, Trinidad and numerous other wealthy importers.

Mr Kenneth Alley, a young Londoner who is managing director, told me that a considerable quantity of merchandise that was not shipped abroad direct, did find its way to other countries in another form eventually, after it had been used by English manufacturing clothiers.

I questioned him as to why deliveries were not made to the all-important dollar countries – America and Canada – and Mr Alley quickly replied that although the English prices of elastic braid were slightly below that being made in those particular countries, there was not sufficient to warrant shipping it over. 'If there was real incentive to sell to those dollar areas, the gap would very quickly close,' he said.

Since the factory opened, production has increased six times and by means of a three eight-hour shift system, between 11 and 12 hundred gross yards of elastic is turned out, the equivalent of 100 miles! Seventeen local girls, all highly skilled, manage the day shift, while a small team of men are engaged upon night work. Their factory manager is Mr R. Wileman, who has had many years of experience in the industry.

I was surprised to learn that Narrow Fabrics Ltd is completely isolated within the industry. There is no similar factory north of Barrow, and the nearest is in the south of Lancashire. The main industry area is the Leicester province.

CHAPTER 3
Ships and Submarines

Barrow shipyard foremen pictured in front of what is believed to be the partly constructed HMS Niobe in 1895.

Shipbuilder to the World

On 28 January 1871 the Barrow Shipbuilding Company was formed at a provisional meeting held in the Abbotswood home of James Ramsden. The company was registered with an authorized capital of £100,000 and seems to have been launched on the sheer enthusiasm of Ramsden rather than on any great technical knowledge of building ships.

It was not an immediate success and its first manager, Mr Robertson, was dismissed in 1876 after the yard made heavy losses. The next manager, James Humphrys, suffered the same fate as the losses continued into the early 1880s. Only the Duke of Devonshire's cash kept the company afloat.

HMS Powerful *in full steam.*

The Naval Construction and Armaments Company Ltd was created in 1888 from the original Barrow Shipbuilding Company. At that time it had 872 workers. When the next big change in name and ownership came in 1897 the business had grown to employ 5,500. In that short space of time the firm had built ships for the Pacific Steam Navigation Company and three liners for the Canadian Pacific.

The British naval cruiser HMS Powerful was the most notable product of the Naval Construction and Armaments Company Ltd. She was the first cruiser built in Barrow and was launched by the Duchess of Devonshire in July 1895. She was built to counter the Russian threat in the Far East but soon became obsolete. Such was her size that special trains brought spectators to Barrow for the launch. She carried a crew of 900 – with room enough for an admiral's suite. The ship weighed in at a mighty 14,200 tons, was 538ft long and could cruise 7,000 miles at 14 knots with a top speed of 22 knots.

HMS Powerful had a short career as a warship. By 1915 she was in use at a Devonport depot and was scrapped at Blyth in 1929. The ship is remembered in the name of a street on Walney.

The Barrow News Almanack *for 1898 described the next stage in the ownership and development of the yard:*

The undertaking of the Naval Construction and Armaments Company was taken over at the end of June 1897 by Vickers, Sons and Company Limited, who also acquired the freehold and property of the Barrow Shipbuilding Company Limited. The two latter companies have since been wound up and Vickers, Sons and Company have since that date taken over the entire concern of the Maxim Nordenfelt Company and the name of the purchasing company has now been altered to Vickers, Sons and Maxim Limited.

This amalgamation of the big concerns under one concentrated company means increased trade for Barrow, inasmuch as the new owners of the Barrow works have within their own resources not only the capacity to build and engine warships of all types, but to equip them with their own renowned armour plates, to mount them with guns which have already won the admiration and approval of the Admiralty officials and supply them with ammunition – in fact to put to sea the most modern types of fighting ships built and equipped from their own resources.

No other firm in the world is in a position to do this but it portends great developments to the shipbuilding trade of Barrow, inasmuch as it will furnish the Barrow yard with a fuller and more comprehensive programme of work at all times, whether trade is good or not, because the new firm will build warships of the type most likely to be required and dispose of them to needy buyers.

Beyond warship construction, Vickers, Sons and Maxim will build all types of commercial tonnage and it is generally expected that their accession to the Barrow yard will lead to a new era of industrial activity in Barrow.

Vickers, Sons and Maxim Limited became Vickers Limited in 1911 during the golden age of warship building in Barrow. The yard built for Japan, Turkey and Brazil as well as great battleships for the British Navy.

Busy Time in Store

This headline hardly sums up the feeling of confidence at a Barrow shipyard which had eleven vessels on the order book. The date was 1936, and with the benefit of hindsight it is easy to see that war was on the way. The Barrow News *of 29 February revealed:*

The Admiralty announces that, subject to the settlement of certain points of detail, they have decided to entrust the construction of the seven tribal class destroyers to the following firms:

Vickers-Armstrongs, Barrow: HMS *Afridi* and *Cossack*. Fairfield Shipbuilding and Engineering, Govan, Glasgow: HMS *Ghurka* and *Maori*. John Thornycroft, Southampton: HMS *Mohawk* and *Nubian*. Alexander Stephens and Sons, Glasgow: HMS *Zulu*.

The seven vessels form the flotilla additional to the normal replacement programme and were provided for the supplementary Naval Estimate recently approved by Parliament. They will be larger and faster than the preceding ships of standard design – 1,375 tons and 37 knots – having a displacements tonnage of 1,850 tons. It has been estimated that they will cost about £400,000 each – £100,000 more than those now under construction.

The ordering of the new flotilla is regarded as the first contribution towards making up the shortage of destroyers under the London Treaty, the deficiency in this class of vessel under the age limit being very great.

We are officially informed that the two destroyers above mentioned will be built at the Barrow yard, where eleven berths will soon be occupied, thus ensuring employment for a large body of men for many months to come.

Cloth caps and bicycles at the end of the shift at Vickers in the 1950s.

The Era of the Sailing Ships

Today Vickers is the name most closely associated with shipbuilding in Barrow but it was not the first to produce vessels in the town. That honour belongs to the Barrow firm of William Ashburner and the first ship off the slipway was the schooner *Jane Roper*.

William was one of ten children of farmer Thomas Ashburner of Gameswell, near Ulverston, and was born in 1809. His career took him first as an apprentice to the Ulverston yards of Petty and Postlethwaite and then to the Isle of Man. He moved to Fisher Street, Barrow, in 1847 at a time when the arrival of the railway and the iron industry were about to transform the whole district.

The new shipyard became known as the Barrow Patent Slip and had space for a single ship to be built close to the Hindpool Farm estate. Its first work was ship repairs until the cash could be raised to build a new vessel. The 105-ton two-masted schooner *Jane Roper* was launched on 15 September 1852.

Schooners were built at Barrow, Ulverston, Greenodd and Millom and were the workhorses of the coastal shipping trade – carrying everything from iron ore to pit props. It was five years before the next Ashburner ship, *Tom Roper,* was launched in July 1857. The third schooner was the *Lord Muncaster,* launched in 1859.

Ashburners launched its first three-masted schooner, the *R. & M.J. Charnley,* in May 1868. It could carry 280 tons. By 1880 Ashburners was employing around 100 men and the working day was from 6 a.m. to 6 p.m. The last schooner from the Ashburner yard was the *J. & M. Garratt* in April 1884. The yard closed soon after.

Some of the Ashburner ships proved themselves against the test of time. The schooner *James Postlethwaite* was built in 1881 and was wrecked in 1954 shortly after appearing in the film *Moby Dick*.

Farmer's Son to Ship Owner

The shipping line James Fisher and Sons started life in 1847 to cater to the growth of the Furness iron mining industry. The Fishers were already a long established Furness family involved in mine ownership and as agents for carting iron ore to the Barrow jetties.

James Fisher was only twenty-four and a farmer's son when he started his company. Today, only the famous P&O line is older than James Fisher's in the ranks of British shipping firms. The founder died in 1873.

The company prospered and was soon running a fleet of more than 100 vessels, mostly two- and three-masted schooners. There were also flats, luggers, brigs, brigantines and barques. The company added steel schooners to its wooden ships in 1886 and soon had its first steamers, ranging from 350 tons to 650 tons.

Best known of the Fishers who ran the company was Sir John Fisher. He was called back to control the company during Army service on the Somme during the First World War. He co-ordinated the company's

This three-masted barque was soon to become a relic of the good old days when this picture was taken around 1895 in Ramsden Dock.

Shipping firm founder James Fisher. His firm was started in 1847 and still thrives to this day.

A Submarine Pioneer

Barrow's close connections with the development of Royal Navy submarines dates to 1900 when the Admiralty ordered five Holland Class submersible craft. They were named after an Irishman, Mr J.D. Holland, who produced his first 14ft submarine in 1878. Each was to measure 63ft in length, be capable of 8 knots on the surface or 5 knots submerged and to have a submerged displacement of 120 tons. The tiny boats could be picked up and launched by a giant 150-ton shipyard crane and when they went to sea with a crew of seven they were armed with a single torpedo tube in the bow. Holland class *Number 1* was launched by Vickers on 2 October 1901 and was built under licence in accordance with patents from the Electric Boat Company of America.

Early submarines often got into difficulties and many lives were lost in peace-time explosions, sinkings and collisions. One of those unfortunate boats was the sixth Holland-class sub, the *A1*. It had been modified into a 100ft submarine with greater speed both on the surface and submerged. It was launched at Barrow on 9 July 1902 but two years later was the subject of the country's first underwater tragedy. *A1* ran into the SS *Berwick Castle* during a training exercise and eleven submariners were killed. Despite this a dozen more A-class submarines had been built by 1905.

The *A1* proved to be a great survivor. The boat was salvaged and recommissioned only to sink again with further loss of life while on trials in 1911. The wreck was rediscovered in 1988, lying under 50ft of water in the Solent.

The proudest record of a Barrow-built submarine probably belongs to Thunderbolt-

contribution to the war effort – the import of iron ore from Spain and Norway to keep the thirty-five blast furnaces between Carnforth and Workington in production. After the war he guided the company in the final changeover from sail to steam. The last sailing ship in the Fisher fleet was the *British Queen* which was sold in 1924. In the Second World War he went to the Ministry of War Transport as director of the coasting and short sea division. Two of the most difficult operations he was to be involved with were Operation Dynamo – the evacuation of the British Expeditionary Force from Dunkirk – and Operation Neptune – the nautical part of the 1944 Normandy landings.

He was knighted in 1942 for his services to the war effort.

class submarine HMS *Turbulent*. It was launched in Barrow in May 1941 and was lost with all hands off Corsica in 1943. Before then it had established a fearsome reputation for sinking a cruiser, a destroyer, a U-boat and twenty-eight transport ships. The commander of the *Turbulent*, John Wallace 'Tubby' Linton, was awarded the Victoria Cross for valour.

The earliest submarines to be built at Barrow were not for the Royal Navy but were the product of a collaboration between the Barrow Shipbuilding Company and the Swedish inventor Nordenfelt. A 100ft long steam-powered Nordenfelt submarine was launched in Barrow on 14 April 1886. A second Nordenfelt was launched in 1887 to a similar design and was sold to Russia.

It ran ashore during the trip and had to be broken up.

The Bigger they Are the Harder they Fall

In 1880 Barrow was thinking big. The Barrow Shipbuilding Company was piecing together the SS *City of Rome* – then the largest passenger liner in the world. It was being built for the Inman Line which ran a service between Liverpool and New York. Inman had lost the speed record for the journey in 1879 and needed a ship of style and distinction to win it back.

The *City of Rome* was job number 77 for

An early Holland Class submarine being lifted on the shipyard's 150-ton electric lifting crane around 1905.

A self-docking, floating ship dock built for Montreal and named the Duke of Connaught.

the Barrow Shipbuilding Company and on the official invitations to the launch on 4 June 1881 the ship was said to be 586ft long, producing 10,000hp and weighing in at 8,826 tons. Special trains brought spectators from Carlisle, Whitehaven, Leeds and Preston. Perhaps 30,000 people visited for this special day and crowded the shoreline twelve rows deep. The launch was arranged for 11 a.m., but ten minutes before then the boiler exploded throwing large pieces of metal hundreds of yards. Four workers were killed but the show went on. At 1 p.m. Lady Clarence Stanley cracked a bottle of champagne on the bow.

Inside the ship everything was designed to provide the height of luxury for the passengers. The dining room could take 248 people at a single sitting and there was space for up to 300 emigrants. In theory the *City of Rome* could make 18 knots but heavy iron plates used instead of the specified steel kept the heavy ship too low in the water to perform like the record-breaker she was supposed to be.

The Inman line did not want the new ship and it was returned to Barrow for a refit and eventual sale to the Anchor Line.

Across the Pacific 315 Times

The *Empress of Japan* was one of three passenger ships built in Barrow for the Canadian Pacific Railway by the Barrow Shipbuilding Company. The ship made 315 crossings of the Pacific in a career lasting more than thirty years.

The ship had been ordered in October 1889 and was launched on 13 December 1890 by Lady Muncaster before starting her maiden voyage twelve days later. The *Empress of Japan* had 118 saloon, 48 second cabin and 500 steerage passengers. She could get close to 19 knots at top speed and could also carry 4,400 tons of cargo on trips lasting up to ten days. The ship was broken for scrap in the 1920s.

Launch of the Empress of China

The Barrow Herald *of 28 March 1891 recorded the spectacle as the* Empress of China *went down the slipway at Barrow.*

The third and last of the vessels which have been built for the Canadian Pacific Railway Co. by the Naval Construction and Armaments Company was launched in glorious weather on Wednesday morning. There was the usual large attendance of sightseers who seemed deeply absorbed in discussing the fine appearance of the vessel.

The *Empress of China* has been constructed on exactly the same lines as the *Empress of India* and *Empress of Japan*, and she was christened on Wednesday by Lady Northcote who performed the function in a very graceful manner.

The stage which had been constructed near the stern was gaily bedecked with flags in honour of the occasion, and when every preparation had been made for her acquaintance with her native element, she was allowed to glide down the incline amid three ringing cheers given by those who were upon the deck. The bystanders responded with a hearty waving of hats, and a moment later the vessel plunged into the channel.

The launch ceremony being over, the invited guests subsequently met in the drawing office where success to the *Empress of China* and her builders was drunk with enthusiasm. Amongst those present were Lady Edward Cavendish, Lady Taunton, Lady Egerton, Lady Northcote, Hon. V. Cavendish, Sir Stafford Northcote, Mr J.A. Duncan MP, Sir James Ramsden, Mr Bryce-Douglas, Mr Charlton, Mr Adamson, Mr Barlow-Massicks, Mr Major (magistrate clerk) and Alderman Wadham. Mr Bryce-Douglas proposed the toast of 'Success to the *Empress of China*' and coupled with it the name of Captain Kellett. Captain Kellett responded and said they would all admit what fine ships the company were capable of turning out.

He had been connected with ships for some time, and was particularly proud of the one they had launched that day. Without doubt every effort would be put forward to make her a success throughout.

Fire sweeps the Empress of Russia

A disastrous fire swept the liner *Empress of Russia* as she lay in Barrow's Buccleuch Dock on 8 September 1945. Two crewmen were killed and the entire dock was enveloped in clouds of smoke. Fire crews battled for four hours to get the flames under control as the ship blazed from bow to stern. At 4 a.m. the whole dock was glowing as flames leapt to the top of the ship's funnels. Water sprayed on the ship's side simply turned to steam due to the intense heat of the burning vessel. The giant ship started to list badly so the level of water in the dock was lowered to prevent a capsize. Firemen arrived at Barrow from as far afield as Kirkby Lonsdale and Preston to help tackle the blaze.

Fire damage to the Empress of Russia *in Barrow docks.*

Saviour of the Convoy

The *Jervis Bay* went into naval folklore during the Second World War when it was sunk in November 1940 during a valiant but suicidal defence of a merchant convoy. As an escort vessel it took on the German pocket battleship *Admiral Scheer*, allowing a merchant convoy to scatter to safety. *Jervis Bay*'s Captain Fogarty was awarded the Victoria Cross posthumously as his ship steamed towards the *Admiral Scheer*, still firing as it sank. A total of thirty-two of the thirty-eight ships in the Atlantic convoy escaped, largely as a result of the *Jervis Bay*'s battle against impossible odds.

Jervis Bay was launched in Barrow in January 1922 and was designed for the Australian Commonwealth Government Line. It changed hands twice and in the winter of 1939 was fitted as a merchant cruiser with eight 6-inch and two 3-inch guns.

Pride of the Brazilian Navy

The *São Paolo* was a powerful battleship built for Brazil to counter the threat of new ships ordered by Chile. She was laid down in June 1907, launched in 1909 and fitted out in Buccleuch Dock. On completion in July 1910 the ship had formidable fire-power. There were twelve massive 12-inch guns, thirty smaller guns and four torpedo tubes. *São Paolo* was 530ft in length and was driven by two sets of triple-expansion engines giving a speed on trials of 21.6 knots. The normal load of coal for the boilers was 800 tons but it could carry up to 2,350 tons for long patrols. At a steady 10 knots she had a steaming range of 10,000 miles. It took 900 men to crew the *São Paolo* and the ship cost £1,821,400 to build.

She was finally decommissioned in 1946.

The Best Cruiser Afloat

Kongo was launched on 18 May 1912 amid a shower of confetti from a balloon suspended from the bow. The ship had been ordered to provide a prototype to build from in the inexperienced Japanese shipyards. At the time it was the best battle cruiser afloat and was rebuilt and improved in the late 1930s. *Kongo* was laid down in 1911 and was designed to be 740ft in length and carry a crew of 1,437. It cost £2,500,000 and hit a trial speed of just over 27 knots. Weaponry included eight 14-inch guns and eight torpedo tubes. *Kongo* was sunk by a United States submarine off north-west Formosa in 1944.

From Barrow to Dunkirk

The TSS *Manxman* started life as an Isle of Man ferry but in 1939 was requisitioned as a troop transport and served at Dunkirk. *Manxman* was launched in Barrow on 15 June 1904 for the Midland Railway.

The 2,174-ton ferry was 334ft long and could manage almost 23 knots from three Parsons turbines. She worked on the Heysham to Douglas route and saw war service from 1915 to 1918 when used by the Admiralty as an auxiliary aircraft carrier.

In 1920 TSS *Manxman* was bought by the Steam Packet Company and converted to burn oil. She was later renamed *Caduceus*

The battleship *São Paolo* was built for the Brazilian navy. 'It looked a treat lit up,' claimed the postcard sender in July 1910.

The launch of the HIJMS Kongo for the Japanese navy on 18 May 1912.

The Great Western Railway steamer SS Roebuck was built at Barrow by the Naval Construction and Armament Company.

by the Admiralty and used as a radar training ship. After two years spent carrying repatriated prisoners of war from Harwich to the Hook of Holland she was scrapped in 1949.

Explosion and Fire at Sea

In December 1914 a disastrous explosion and fire struck an oil ship called the *Vedra* which later ran aground off Walney. It was reported that the ship was enveloped in fierce flames which led to the death of thirty-five crew members.

'Before any of the crew practically had time to look about, they were surrounded by furious tongues of flame,' the *North-Western Daily Mail* reported.

Only two crew members survived the initial blast and subsequent blaze. One later died in hospital. A few days later, James Dixon was well enough to describe his ordeal. He believed the fire started below decks and told how he raced through flame-filled passageways and suffered burns to his face. He said: 'When we got up above we saw sailors jumping overboard.'

He went over the side into the freezing water and watched as the tug boat *Furness* and the Barrow lifeboat battled to get close in rough weather.

The *Vedra* was heading to Barrow from Texas carrying 6,000 tons of highly inflammable benzine.

Armoured cruiser HMS King Alfred *was launched in 1901.*

Tragic Loss of the Vanguard

The biggest disaster to befall a Barrow-built ship concerned the huge dreadnought HMS *Vanguard*. It was originally laid down in Barrow in April 1908 as the *Rodney*. The ship cost £1,607,780 and on delivery to the Royal Navy in March 1910, it had become *Vanguard* – sister ship of the *St Vincent* and the *Collingwood*.

The *Vanguard* was part of the fourth battle squadron at Jutland – the most famous naval battle of the First World War – but the ship's luck was not to last. On 9 July 1917, 804 men lost their lives when the entire ship exploded at Scapa Flow. Only two of those aboard the ship survived.

The official report said: 'At 23.30 on a fine summer evening in July 1917, when the Battle Fleet was settling down for the night, the *Vanguard* blew up with a shocking explosion which rocked the next ship in line, *Collingwood*, and lit up the whole sky with its glare. In three minutes she had disappeared, leaving behind her an immense column of smoke, some burning oil on the water and a small target at which she had been firing that afternoon in the Flow. Searchlights were turned on the scene and boats were got away, but there were only two survivors from those on board.'

It seems that a number of *Vanguard*'s officers had been attending a sing-song on another ship and were on their way back when the ship exploded. They survived.

The cause is still the subject of controversy. Faulty ammunition could have been to blame but an enemy agent was found to have been a dockyard man on the ship and was said to have been aboard *Vanguard* at 5 p.m. on the day of the explosion.

Daring Rescue Saves a Life

Coastal shipping could be a dangerous business. Small, often aging sailing ships carried everything from iron ore to coal and pit props to and from the Furness coast. When bad weather, bad navigation or just bad luck intervened, shipping accidents often turned into tragedies. The misfortune of the Lunesdale *and the amazing rescue of its captain from what looked like certain death was reported in the* Barrow Herald *of 28 March 1891.*

The Loss of the *Lunesdale*: a Thrilling Experience – We reported briefly the other week the loss of the *Lunesdale*, of Barrow, with four hands, in Start Bay, and made mention of the fact that Captain Jones, of 17 Harley Street, Barrow, was the only hand saved.

From information gleaned, it would appear that the experiences of the captain were of the most thrilling description, and his survival is truly miraculous.

At the time of the disaster, a blinding snow was falling, and it was bitterly cold. Captain Jones, as a last resort, lashed himself to the rigging, whilst the other four attached themselves to the mizzen rigging. For two and a half hours the captain was in this predicament, and as he was wearing little clothing at the time, his limbs were benumbed beyond description.

The mate appears to have held on the longest of the four in the mizzen, and at intervals the captain tried to open a conversation with him, but the replies he made to interrogations were very faint, and absolutely unintelligible.

His fellow seamen, it is supposed, were washed overboard at an early hour by the boiling surf, but as the survivor could not see nor be seen there is no evidence to show how. Later the vessel was washed ashore, and as she was speedily sighted, measures were promptly taken to ascertain whether any of the crew were living. A big burly fisherman was delegated to wade through the water as far as he dare venture, conveying with him a long rope, at one end of which was attached a piece of lead. He observed the captain lashed to the rigging, and threw the rope in the hope of effecting a rescue. The cord dropped at the captain's feet, and in his exhausted state, and when life was rapidly ebbing away, he perceived yet a hope of escape.

With his teeth he unlashed himself, and descended as well as his stiffened limbs would allow, and in due time had grasped the rope and was making the necessary preparations for his next experience. The line having been securely fastened around the body, he threw himself into the water, and was pulled ashore in an utterly unconscious state. It is hardly necessary to state that he was at once removed to an inn, and that prompt measures were resorted to restore the animation that was fast leaving his frame. 'At four o'clock in the morning the ill-fated schooner was split in two, and at daylight only fragments of her were to be seen afloat.

The mate, who belongs to London, leaves a widow and three children to mourn his loss, whilst the other unfortunate creatures who were drowned are reported to be single. One of these belongs to Barrow, whilst one came from Folkestone, and the other from London.

A welcome sight for sailors heading to the safety of Barrow port was the Walney lighthouse, shown here on a 1907 postcard.

CHAPTER 4
Sport and Leisure

The Walney Royal Pierrots were popular entertainers, often performing on the stage in James Dunn Park.

Cash and a Gold Medal

Boxing was a big attraction in the recession years. It offered young men a chance of local celebrity – and cash prizes at a time when work was hard to come by. A typical commercial boxing matinée for the bantam championship of Furness was the focus of a report in the North-Western Daily Mail of 13 March 1920.

Additional interest was lent to Mr Ames's programme at the Palace today by the fact that two of the leading bantam-weights, not only in this district, but in the North, were meeting for £25 aside and Mr Ames's purse of £25, and were also contending for the championship of Furness. A cup at this weight was given by Mr Percy Linton and a gold medal given by Mr Wilf Diamond.

Both are skilful boxers and the keen

interest was reflected in the splendid attendance. The main bout put Nibby Penny against Bert Fitton. It was not to last the distance. The opening was quiet, each sizing the other up. The second also was boxed on quiet lines, Fitton perhaps doing the most leading; but Penny, in the third round, got a nice left home, followed by the right.

'Both were pretty wary and were giving nothing away. In the fourth round there was an unfortunate termination, for Fitton was disqualified for hitting low. The latter was chagrined and claimed he had not committed any offence, but the referee had no doubt on the matter.

A disastrous fire at Barrow's Old Town Hall on 24 March 1931 put the future of boxing in jeopardy. Barrow Boxing Syndicate lost all its uninsured equipment in the fire, which also destroyed the regular venue for fights. Bouts continued at venues round the town, including the Old Drill Hall, the Baths and even at His Majesty's Theatre.

Top Barrow professional boxer, Frank Hill.

Never Knocked Out

One of Barrow's best-known professional boxers was Frank Hill. As a teenager he fought the best lightweights in the North of England, including Alex Alston of Preston, Ginger Roberts of Whitley Bay and Jack Carrick of Hull. He retired in 1938 at the very early age of twenty-three years, after eye trouble.

His record showed 102 fights without suffering a single knock-out. He won forty-six fights on points, eighteen by knock-out or technical knock-out, drew five, lost twenty on points, two on retirements and eight on disqualifications. He very nearly reached the pinnacle of the profession, going to London for twelve months under the wing of Jack Solomans and coming close to a British title bout. The boxing press tagged him 'the great lightweight hope'.

Injury took away his best years but in retirement he was able to pass on his skills as the boxing instructor to the 56th anti-tank battalion. He later became sports officer of the Barrow Navy League Sea Cadets and in the early 1950s took over as Barrow Rugby League trainer.

Support for Swimming Club

Barrow Amateur Swimming Club had fantastic support in 1920, boasting more than 900

A pair of champion swimmers and their coach pose with trophies and medals from a successful season on a picture from around 1920.

members. Its ranks had been swelled by the influx of young munitions workers during the Great War. An end of season report in the North-Western Daily Mail *of 27 February* stated:

Barrow Amateur Swimming Club is in a position to feel exceedingly proud of its flourishing condition. While most clubs of the kind had to be suspended in consequence of the war, the abnormal conditions simply helped to build up the local organization. A satisfactory feature of the Barrow club is the rare healthiness of its junior section. As a matter of fact the only local records broken this year have been broken by juniors.

In all departments the year's happenings have been satisfactory and quite in keeping with the general position of the club, which with its 905 members, is one of the strongest numerically in all England. Financially the club is sounder than ever. The balance in the bank at the commencement of the year of £26 8s has been doubled.

High-Speed Thrills at Walney

On Easter Monday in 1925 huge crowds were drawn to Walney for timed motorcycle road trials at Biggar Bank. Furness District Motor Sports Club organized the trials in the early 1920s before road racing was banned. The racers were Barrow men and one of them, Frank Charles, went on to become a professional rider. The motorcyclists raced on the sands at North Scale for a year or two after the road ban, but races were then moved to Southport where there was a longer stretch of sand.

The Joys of the Open Road

Motorcycling at a rather more sedate pace was both a popular pastime and a common means of transport when cars were still a relatively rare sight and out of the reach of most pockets. Shown on the photograph is Barrovian Fred Edge. His son Brian, who kindly provided the photograph, now lives near Crewe. The machine he sits on is a Dunelt of around 1928 and it has the distinctive Barrow registration plate EO3841 and carbide lighting. The Dunelt was a British machine and at that period there was almost 200 motorcycle manufacturers in the country.

A flat cap and a pipe were essential equipment for the motorcyclist of the 1920s. Here Fred Edge is shown on his Dunelt.

Barrow always produced its fair share of sporting stars. Shown here is Harry Gifford, the Barrow and Lancashire Northern Rugby Union full-back.

Cup Final Watched by 7,000

It is hard to imagine today the size of the crowds which were regularly drawn to relatively low-key sporting events involving Barrow teams. A good example was the 1920 final of the Ulverston Hospital Cup where Ulverston Town took on the Barrow Shipbuilders before 7,000 spectators! The North-Western Daily Mail *on 13 March described the action:*

For this interesting cup final the Education Authority granted the use of the Victoria Grammar School field and there was a record crowd of 7,000 spectators, including a big invasion of the followers of the 'Ships'. The playing of the Ulverston Town Band livened the proceedings and a fine, open, stubbornly contested game delighted the crowd.

Ulverston: Tait, Collinson and Bamber, Downham, Williams and Mackintosh, Jarvis, Atkinson, Smith, Pearce and Yates.

Shipbuilders: Kendall, Larner and Fitzgerald, Rigg, Wardropper and Greenway, Spencer, Brough, Mawson, Proudfoot and Fletcher.

The ground was heavy, but following heavy rains the weather had fortunately cleared when Mawson started for the Shipbuilders. The game opened fast and even, and soon Smith put in a lovely shot. Ulverston pressed for some time and showed good form, Smith tricking an opponent and scoring a beautiful goal.

The Ships then attacked and had hard lines. The town came again and Fitzgerald cleared in fine style. Later Yates centred and Atkinson scored. Shot after shot was then rained on the Ships goal, but without avail.

On crossing over at half-time, the Ships again became aggressive but were weak in front of goal. They continued, however, to press strongly and ultimately Spencer scored with a low shot which utterly baffled Tait. Ulverston on returning to the attack were awarded a penalty and Bamber scored. Joe Smith next missed a fine opening but made amends later by a good goal. Downham was badly hurt and had to be carried off. Result: Ulverston four, Shipbuilders one.

Councillor Chapman, chairman of the council, presented the cup to the victors.

A Soccer Star in the Making

Big things were expected in 1920 of Barrow soccer player William Douglas who merited his own profile in the North-Western Daily Mail *of March 27 in 1920.*

A lad who has come prominently to the front this season in the ranks of the Barrow soccer team is William Douglas, right half, who has worthily maintained his place in the team, and promises to develop greater skill and resource even yet.

Born in Manchester in 1897, he is the son of a footballer, his father Ernest J. Douglas having played left half-back for Manchester City in that club's earlier days. William has been in Barrow ten years, having served his apprenticeship with Vickers. He played for Vickerstown School for a season and was in the Walney Parish team when war broke out. He also played for the Walney Scouts as centre forward, scoring fifteen goals in fourteen matches.

'Four-and-a-half years ago he threw in his lot with Barrow AFC, but has not been a regular member of the first team until this season. Douglas is a keen athlete, being fond of cricket, swimming and walking. He is one of the lads who has made good in local football.

Victory at Wembley Stadium

No brief survey of Barrow's sporting past is complete without mention of the famed Rugby League Challenge Cup winners of 1955.

Saturday 30 April was the big day. Much of the town had left for Wembley Stadium by special buses and trains to see Barrow become national cup winners for the first time. The cup was received by Barrow captain Willie Horne from the Duke of Edinburgh after the victory over Workington Town by 21 points to 12.

Barrow Rugby League returned to Barrow on Monday and the players were greeted by a crowd of 15,000 people at the Craven Park ground. The victorious team was Best, Lewthwaite, Jackson, P. Goodwin, Castle, Willie Horne, Toohey, Belshaw, McKeating, Barton, Grundy, Parker and Healey. Leatherbarrow and J. Wilson were reserves.

Still Proud in Defeat

On 7 May in 1938 Barrow had also reached the Wembley Challenge Cup final but the result went to Salford by seven points to four. This was the first Barrow Rugby League team to reach the final and they returned as heroes. At the civic reception held for the team, Barrow RFC chairman John Atkinson said: 'If we did not bring back the cup, we feel that honour is only delayed.'

The welcome crowds started at Hawcoat Lane and at the station corner it was

A Barrow women's hockey team pose for town photographer J. Parker around 1910.

impossible to move. From there to the town hall the road was lined four or five deep with well-wishers. 'I do not know what kind of reception we would have got if we had brought back the cup. The way people have turned out is marvellous,' Mr Atkinson told guests at the civic reception. The players appeared on the town hall balcony to receive cheers and applause.

Alex Troup was the captain and the other team members were French, Cumberbatch, Higgin, McDonnel, Thornburrow, Lloyd, Little, Rawlings, McKeating, Skelly, Ayres and Markhew.

When Barrow beat Leeds in the quarter-final at Craven Park they were watched by a crowd of 20,000. It was the first match when the club had exceeded £1,000 in gate money. As losing finalists at Wembley the Barrow players received £5 each – normal winning pay was £3 for an away win, £2 for a draw and £1 5s for a defeat.

First Past the Post Gets £40

While Barrow still had plenty of wide open spaces it was not unusual to find a crowd in a field and two or more horsemen racing for pride – and a side-bet. The Barrow Times *of 12 July 1879 reported on one such 'galloping race at Barrow'.*

A great deal of interest was manifested in a galloping match on the Race Grounds, Newbarns, on Monday evening, between Mr W. Kendall's Dr Kenealy and Mr Patterson's Spider, for a stake of £40. Both horses have won the Cartmel Hunt Plate, Dr Kenealy being the victor in 1878, and Spider carrying off the prize this year. Joseph Richardson rode Spider, whilst J. Rawcliffe Jnr piloted Dr Kenealy.

A good start was made, Dr Kenealy going to the front with a lead of two lengths, which at the west end of the course was increased by an additional length. On passing a point near the Strawberry, Mr Kendall's horse took the rails, and at once lost all chance of winning, although Rawcliffe managed to keep his seat. Spider then went to the front and had the race all its own way, Rawcliffe having given up. Mr W. Boulton acted as judge and starter.

Birth of a Soccer Club

A packed meeting at Barrow Drill Hall saw the birth of Barrow AFC on 16 July 1901. Old football professional Moses Saunders was enlisted to recruit and train players. During the meeting Mr J.H. Hind called for 2,000 members to pay 2s 6d for season tickets. It was hoped that this would produce £80 to buy a field and £170 for players.

Barrow AFC won the first match against Blackpool by three goals to one. The second match, against Chorley in the Lancashire Cup, attracted 3,302 spectators. On 28 September the new team had its first match against a League team, Sheffield Wednesday.

The Stars Come Out

Smaller football clubs have always made ends meet by selling the occasional player to the Football League clubs. In 1921 Barrow AFC lost a player to mighty Everton, but they did get a match against the big boys as part of the transfer deal. The North-Western Daily Mail *of 5 April reported on the friendly game – where Barrow emerged victorious.*

As part of the bargain for the transfer of Alford, Everton sent a fairly representative team to Barrow last night and a crowd estimated at between 6,000 and 7,000 assembled at Holker Street to witness what proved to be an interesting game.

Barrow, who were at full strength, won after a meritorious struggle by 2-0 and the spectators

The crowds turned out to watch Barrow AFC take on the mighty Everton on 4 April 1921.

went away after the match quite pleased with what they had seen. The game, although lacking in those exciting thrills usually to be found in League games, afforded some idea of what we may expect from Barrow next season when they appear in the League.

They were playing against experienced men in this game, each of whom is capable of taking his place in first class football. Five of the visitors, indeed, have played in First League matches this season – Wall (inside left), Parker (centre forward), Kirksopp (outside right), Livesley (centre half) and Robinson (left back). It was expected that H. Howard Baker, the champion high jumper, would defend the Everton goal, but his place was taken by Salt.

Barrow's defence was exceedingly good, the halves never allowing the Everton forwards much rope and McKay was specially reliable at full back. The home forwards did not show their best. Matthews for a long time was unable to make much impression on Jones, whose half back play was brilliant. Later on the Barrow right winger showed up better. The forward play on both sides was lacking cohesion, the light ball being difficult to control but in defensive play both sides shone. Alford, the ex-Barrow player, was never much in the picture, except for his off-side tactics. Barrow received £450 plus last night's gate for this young player, so that the club has done well out of him and will wish him every success.

Final Curtain Falls

Barrow lost its last theatre on 12 April 1968 when the curtains went down for the final time at Her Majesty's Theatre in Albert Street. Music-hall stars and theatrical companies had entertained thousands of Barrovians at the theatre since it opened in 1905. Debts had mounted after the Second World War and the theatre closed owing more than £3,000. It used to have its own repertory company, the Saxon Players, and held variety shows.

Before Queen Elizabeth came to the throne the theatre was know as His Majesty's and an old theatre programme from 1950 shows that the Saxon Players were presenting the new musical comedy *Let's Face the Music*. From Boxing Day 1950 to 6 January 1951 the show could be seen twice nightly at 6.30 p.m. and 8.40 p.m. with tickets for the cheapest pit stalls being 1s 6d for adults and 1s for children. The show's producer was Bruce Fisk and the cast included Duncan Robertson, Mary Dawson, Douglas Hayes and Valerie Pearson – who appeared in the film *A Boy, a Girl and a Bike*.

Hollywood Nights in Barrow

There was no shortage of places in Barrow to escape daily life for an hour or two and enter the world of Hollywood make-believe. The Coliseum, Ritz and Odeon were seen as the town's luxury houses of cinema entertainment. In Duke Street the Palace was billed as 'the people's favourite', but the oldest purpose-built cinema of them all was the Electric, which closed in 1957. Other cinemas were the Gaiety, later called the Essoldo, the Regal, the Pavilion, the Royal and the Walney. Movies also made an appearance at other venues, including His Majesty's Theatre.

The Height of Modern Style

The site of the old Roxy cinema in Cavendish Street has been a place of

Enjoying a slice of Hollywood at the Roxy cinema in Cavendish Street, Barrow, around 1938.

entertainment since the very early days of Barrow. The Royalty Music Hall was given approval in 1871 – one of the first sets of plans to be considered by the borough surveyor's department. In 1875 the building was improved and became the Alhambra. It went back to its original name in 1909 and was providing music hall acts and theatre until April 1937.

August 1937 saw the arrival of the modern picture palace, an art deco temple to the Hollywood stars of the movies. The Roxy was entirely modern in both building style and equipment – its neon lighting was among the finest in the region and its entrance hall and foyer were panelled in Australian walnut. There was a full house of 1,000 people on the first night to see Errol Flynn and Olivia de Havilland in *The Charge of the Light Brigade*. Souvenir brochures said the cinema decoration 'represents an entirely new departure in interior treatment. It can be described as a modern version of Italian Renaissance.'

A *Barrow News* reporter, who was there for the first night, wrote: 'The Roxy is the very latest thing in cinemas, a description which means a great deal nowadays. Architects and the men of the building trade have waved a magic wand. They have plied their pencils, their trowels, their hammers and their brushes to excellent effect. They have worked with the ideal of comfort and luxury always in mind and the result is not only a splendid cinema, but a fine addition to a busy shopping centre.'

The Roxy was owned by James Brennan, one of the leading showmen in the county. It added to his entertainment empire which included the Roxy cinemas at Carnforth, Dalton and Ulverston, the Palladium and St George's Theatre at Kendal and the Verona at Knott End. In later years the old cinema became Champers nightclub and part of the building has now been converted to shops.

The Organist Entertains

The Apollo on the corner of Abbey Road and Holker Street was the last of the traditional Barrow cinemas to close – making way for a new multiplex venue at Hollywood Park. It started life as the Ritz but has also been known as the Astra and the ABC. The Ritz was officially opened by Alderman Bram Longstaffe in September 1936. The film shown was It's Love Again, starring Jessie Matthews. It was equipped with the latest high-intensity arcs and modern projectors with Western Electric Wide Range Sound.

The new cinema even had a swish Ritz Café serving morning coffee, luncheon, tea and supper. One of its more notable attractions was a Compton organ which took ten years to develop. It could play music for concerts and dancing – it could even reproduce the sounds of Big Ben, the bells of St Martins-in-the Fields and great bell carillons such as those at Bruges and Malines.

Figures don't Add Up

One of the hardest losses to suffer was the slow and sorry demise of the Coliseum, which once stood proudly on the corner of Abbey Road and Rawlinson Street. In 1976 the council accepted a tender of £2,984 to demolish a fine building for which no financially viable use could be found. The 1,000-seater cinema and theatre had finally shut in 1964. The last film, shown on 18 January was Against All Flags, *starring Errol Flynn and Maureen O'Mara. In an Evening Mail diary column from 20 January that year the reasons for closure were plain to see:*

As a centre of film and theatrical entertainment, the Coliseum, Barrow, is no more. Stage shows and films at the imposing white-faced, green-domed building which dominates the Rawlinson Street, Abbey Road junction now pass into the realms of memory. Nobody with the authority to say so has yet declared that the Coliseum is to be closed permanently but it seems a certain bet that its fate is irrevocably sealed. The pattern is all too clear.

Filmland's dashing heroes, the principal boys of pantomime, Barrow's amateur actors – all have made their final bows at the Coli. Built after the 1914-18 war, the Coliseum lived on for nearly half-a-century, surviving a fire in the process. But it cannot survive present-day economic pressures and the decline in audiences. People today have more money for entertainment but tastes have changed and those who still go to the cinema and the live theatre demand not only the supreme kind of comfort but the top-line show, too.

There are many cinemas which have to take second-best or very old films. Audience-pulling films go to the big, modern houses. The sad truth is that establishments like the Coliseum cannot compete with the better cinemas with the better programmes, or with television,

A 1972 view of the Barrow Coliseum theatre and cinema before the demolition crew moved in.

bingo and club life. There are many such poorly supported places of entertainment throughout the country, all catering for sparse audiences. There are many which have been closed and the Coliseum is now unhappily in fashion.

Many Barrovians will have nostalgic memories of childhood visits to the Coliseum. They will remember the joys of those unsophisticated days when they found genuine thrills in the adventures of the celluloid pirates and cowboys, the invincible heroes of the screen. But reality has to be faced. The Barrow public don't want the Coliseum as a cinema, or a theatre. As such it now becomes part of the town's history.

Regal Goes for New Town Centre

Most of Barrow's old places of entertainment went with a whimper. The Regal cinema joined them in the history books but at least its supporters put up a fight. The Forshaw Street building closed in December 1956 and vanished – along with much of the rest of the street – to make way for town centre redevelopment. It had started life in 1868 as a music hall and was thought worthy of a Grade II listing because of its architectural merit. The Ancient Monuments Society and the Barrow Civic Society spoke out in defence of the building, but years of decay left little to save.

A whisky label from the Barrow brewers and spirit blenders James Thompson.

The Story of the Barrow Brewers

The Burlington Brewery on the Strand was the town's first commercial brewing venture. It had started life as a brewhouse for the Burlington Hotel. By 1861 it was in the ownership of James Tyson and had started to build up a group of public houses to sell its beers. The fate of the brewery was settled in 1884 as the council wanted the site to make way for the High Level Bridge. At that time the brewery could produce up to sixty barrels of beer per week.

The Sun Brewery stood on land behind the Sun Hotel in Paradise Street. By the early 1870s it was capable of producing up to fifty barrels per week and a year later was known as the Important Fact Brewery. It was run by the Barrow Brewery Company until 1885 when it closed and the equipment was offered for sale.

Another of the small-scale brewers was the Welcome Brewery in Church Street. It was established in 1858 by John Mashiter. It could produce up to thirty barrels per week but was closed by 1873.

Cases' Brewery on Cavendish was one of the best known and certainly the longest lasting of the Barrow beer producers. It was built around 1867 for Thwaites and Hindle but was bought by R.F. Case on 19 August 1867. Robert Case's New Brewery was described by the Barrow Times as the most modern in the North West. It was run by the Case family until 1959 when Geoffrey Case sold the brewery, fifty-two public houses and ten off-licences to Hammonds United Breweries of Yorkshire, which through merger eventually became part of the Bass Charrington empire.

Heath's Devonshire Brewery on Hindpool Road won approval from Barrow Council in 1879 and was designed and equipped by Pontifex of London. It stayed in family control until 1959 when Hammonds took it over and ended beer production in January 1960.

James Thompson had a small brewery next to the Welcome Inn in Barrow but sold it in 1873 as his beer was supplied until 1928 by the Whittle Springs Brewery at Chorley. Thompson's then brewed at Heaths in Barrow and after 1932 with Hartley at Ulverston. In 1966 the Thompson bottling plant, offices and forty-eight licensed premises were sold to Whitbreads. For three years the name lived on as Whitbread-Thompsons until the bottling plant and offices closed in 1969 and the Thompson name vanished.

Roll Out the Barrel

The *1898 News Almanack* for Barrow offered beer not by the pint but by the barrel.

George S. Heath, the brewer, wine and spirit merchant of Hindpool Road, Barrow, boasted a 'choice selection of wine and spirits of the best brands always in stock.' Its speciality whiskies included King's Blend, Roe's Five Year Old, Glen Blend and Cuidich An Righ. Invalid stout and light dinner ale in screw stoppered bottles cost 1s 4d a dozen. If you wanted to buy in bulk Duke's Very Strong Ale was £1 10s for a kilderkin – that's 18 gallons!

In the same booklet you could try Thompson's Coca Wine, described as a cure for everything from insomnia to a nervous disposition. James Thompson's, better known later for its fizzy pop, was based at 237 Dalton Road and at bonded stores on Devonshire Dock, and advised use of its tonic by the wine glass before or with each meal. The company even found a former principal of the Liverpool College of Chemistry to help promote the beneficial use of the extract of the coca leaf.

Granville Sharpe claimed:

'I hereby certify that I have submitted to a very searching chemical analysis, samples of the Coca Wine, as supplied by Mr James Thompson, Barrow-in-Furness, and from the results obtained I can express a very favourable opinion as to the skilful manner in which it has been prepared, and its value as a nerve tonic and in cases of depressed vitality and general debility. It is a highly concentrated product, obtained from the choicest and purest materials and in the selection of which every care has been exercised. It contains, in a particularly agreeable and palatable form, valuable restorative and sustaining principles, and in cases of nervous prostration, brain fag, physical fatigue, sleeplessness and lowness of the spirits, it will be found a valuable, effective and reliable preparation.'

Thompson's was also the sole proprietor of old highland whiskies such as Abbey Brand, Liner Brand and Piel Brand. It held large stocks of Havana, Mexican and British cigars and kept twenty-year-old vintage brandy.

The Last Barrow Pint

On 2 March 1972 Barrow-brewed beer became a thing of the past. The last barrels were rolled out from Case's Cavendish Street brewery before the doors were shut forever. The 100-year-old brewery had fallen victim to big business economies of scale – the same

The Victoria Park Hotel on Victoria Road, Barrow, in 1907.

way hundreds of local and regional breweries had gone before.

Owners Bass Charrington, who took over the firm from the Case family in 1959, came to the conclusion that it was cheaper to transport beer from Liverpool and Runcorn to Barrow.

Case's black and potent Best Mild was considered the premier local tipple. Back in 1938 Barrow News advertisements for the brewery offered Mild ale at 6s for twelve large bottles with Imperial Pale Ale or Nut Brown costing a little more at 7s for a dozen.

Where's All the Beer Gone?

It doesn't matter how friendly the pub is or even how good is the reputation of the local brewery – if there is no beer to be had. In the North-Western Daily Mail of 12 May in 1919 a letter under the name 'Pro bono publico' complained about a 'Beerless Barrow':

Barrow on Saturday night was practically beerless, consequent on a very general closing of the doors of the public houses. The country has been led to believe that there would be more and better beer, but apart from this I suggest that it is high time that the chief constable and the proper authorities in Barrow saw to it that the licence-holders of this town should no longer be allowed to play ducks and drakes with the public rights of the people in regard to the facilities for the consumption of drink.

Like a good many other people in trade, the licensed victualler has become very independent as the result of inflated profits. It is high time they were made to understand that a licence is granted them to conduct their places as refreshment houses, not solely to meet the requirements of the public during regulation hours.

I can point to several public houses in Barrow whose doors were closed on Saturday night, but which were open at dinner-time on Sunday, so it cannot be argued that it was by reason of shortage of supply. I see by the papers that Mr Will Thorne MP, who is a member of the Liquor Control Board, says:

'There are one or two things that the publicans ought to be made to remember. They have done very well, whatever they may say, during the war, and this business of opening and shutting up at uncertain hours at night ought to be adjusted. It has become impossible for the public to know when a house is going to be open, and whether there will be any chance of getting into it when it is.'

And this is just what Barrow has very much to complain of.

Celebration Dinner

The Victoria Park Hotel on Victoria Road finally opened for business in 1902 after eleven years of false dawns. As early as 1891 a licence application had been rejected for a new hotel on Oxford Street. It was to have cost £3,500. In 1898 plans were at an advanced stage to start building the Victoria Park Hotel on the corner of Oxford Street and Brighton Street. It was refused a licence and the developers had to wait until the following year to be granted a provisional licence. The hotel was to cost £5,000 and be equipped with a bowling green and stables.

The new hotel celebrated the completion of building work on 18 February 1902 when Barrow brewer James Thompson held a celebratory dinner at the Royal Hotel. The architects were Currey and

A new-looking King Alfred Hotel at Vickerstown on a postcard from around 1910.

The Duke of Edinburgh Hotel on the corner of Abbey Road and Rawlinson Street, around 1905.

Watson of Newcastle and the official public opening was on 19 April.

A New Pub

The King Alfred Hotel was opened by Earl Grey on 15 February 1904. It had started life on the drawing board in 1899 when the company building the Vickerstown estate on Walney applied for a licence for a new public house. The plan was to call it the Vickers Arms but the application was turned down as premature.

In 1902 a provisional licence was granted for the King Alfred to a Mrs Parry for the Public House Trust. The architect for the new hotel was Mr W. Moss-Settle and it was built by Thomas Riley of Fleetwood. The King Alfred name is borrowed from HMS *King Alfred*, an armoured cruiser launched in Barrow during October 1901.

Raise a Glass to the Duke

The Duke of Edinburgh Hotel is one of the most prominent buildings in the town, welcoming visitors to the town by road or rail on the strategic corner of Abbey Road and Rawlinson Street. It was built in 1873 at a cost of £13,000 and received its licence in September the following year. The grand new hotel was intended to cater to the needs of people arriving in town at the new Barrow Central Station. In March 1876 the hotel had a setback when proprietor Thomas Martin was declared bankrupt. Business picked up, however, and in 1882 the Duke of Edinburgh was upgraded and extended for the new owner, Mr Twiss.

CHAPTER 5
The Great War

The Union Flags fall to reveal Barrow's memorial to those killed in the First World War. The ceremony on 11 November 1921 drew thousands of people to Barrow Park.

Over by Christmas

Barrow went into the First World War full of national pride and cheerful determination in the summer of 1914. Men signed up in droves, military bands led troops on recruiting parades and everyone thought it would all be over by Christmas. It never quite worked out like that.

Many of those who wanted to 'do their bit' were to be disappointed. Barrow was a major producer of war materials and the big employers were able to refuse consent to essential workers wanting to exchange overalls for uniform. This kept down the proportion of Barrow men killed on the front line in comparison to many towns of a similar size, but hundreds of Barrovians were killed and

Soldiers of No. 3 platoon of the 1/4 King's Own Royal Lancaster Regiment pictured during training in Tonbridge during 1914. How many of them survived the horrors of the First World War?

hundreds more injured or changed forever by their experience of conflict.

As each day went by the local newspapers were filled with news of strategy, maps of ground taken and speeches from military commanders. For reasons of censorship and the need to preserve morale on the home front, editors could not give a true picture of the conditions under which the young men of Furness fought and died. In many ways they did not need to. Daily and weekly papers were packed with pictures and brief life histories of the young men who would not be coming back. Often the best part of a whole page was given over to this.

While people were being killed every day – by bullet, shell, gas, or disease – it was the major offensives which captured the imagination and live on in history. None of these was greater than the First Day of the Somme on 1 July 1916. The battle claimed 500,000 casualties – 60,000 of them on the first day alone. In the *Evening Mail* of 15 July an eye-witness description of the attack was printed from Lance-Corporal Harry Werry, written to his parents at Dalton:

'This is the first opportunity I have had of writing to you since the memorable First of July, when we "went over the top" and drove the Boche from their trenches. I suppose I am still unable to give you any information as to our whereabouts, but when I tell you that we were in the middle of it, and that our division was the first to start the ball rolling you will have a fair idea as to our position. It was a magnificent day for our men, and the Germans who happened to be in front of our lads on that day will never forget it – those of them who are still alive.

It was natural that we should have to pay our toll. George Spiller was wounded in the neck – a side glance from a bullet, but the wound is not serious. He will go to England and have a well-earned rest from it. I saw him on his way to the dressing station.

It was good to see the German prisoners coming in. They had had practically nothing to eat or drink for the last three days preceding our assault owing to the intensity of our artillery fire.'

He went on to write:

'Our lads made a magnificent charge, cleared out three lines of trenches, bombing the dugouts, took prisoners, attained their objective, and consolidated the position.'

Individual soldiers didn't see much of the big picture. Battles were noisy, violent and confusing where success in attacking one part of the enemy defences might be contrasted with abject failure a few hundred yards away, as another letter from the front reported: 'We all went over like one man, but got caught in the machine gun fire, and were mown down like corn.'

Back in Barrow the conflicting needs of the arms industry and the military for men led to crisis. By September 1916 the need for new army recruits was so dire that a Barrow tribunal into exemptions from war service dealt with fourteen cases – only five were not sent to France. An *Evening Mail* reporter was told: 'We have got to such a state that single men must be got from somewhere.'

Barrow Builds for Victory

It would be hard to overestimate the role played by Barrow in supporting the war effort between 1914 and 1918. It constructed giant ships for the Royal Navy, held a near monopoly in the

Finishing off shells on the lathes at Vickers. Millions had been produced by the end of the First World War in 1918.

pioneering field of submarine building, produced huge guns for ships and land use and turned out shells by the million. By the middle of 1917 Vickers had turned out 2½ million shells in all shapes and sizes up to an enormous 15-inch diameter. To keep up this vast output in the shipyard and engineering works around 35,000 men and women were kept hard at work – most of them entirely new to war work and many of them untried in any kind of industrial setting. A representative of The Christian Science Monitor described a visit to Vickers in the Ulverston News of 18 August 1917:

To pass in a few hours through works covering many hundreds of acres is to receive an impression of unending masses of metal, endless rows of machines, uncountable piles of shells, and a never-ending din against which background only the broad facts stand out.

This particular workshop town is, for example, home of the submarine. The visitor is treated with flattering frankness and trustfulness, but he is not allowed a glimpse of the inside of these underwater monsters. As a concession, he may be permitted to explore the inwards of the skeleton of a full-sized wooden model. This is interesting enough. This model is constructed with the utmost care, and the different parts are then taken away to the shops, to serve as an exact standard and measure of what is wanted. Thus the model standardises, as it were, the construction of machines of that particular type.

The British effort in the munitions factories has been marked by intensive cultivation, as well as by amplification. From this point of view it was interesting to learn that in the shell department the speeding up in output represents a gain of

The sheer scale is impressive in this view of the gun-mounting department at Vickers-Maxim, around 1904. The outbreak of the First World War brought a fever of activity.

A group of Barrow munitions workers pose at a photographic studio in Paxton Terrace. Many such pictures would be sent home to families of workers forced to go to Barrow for war work between 1914 and 1918.

200 per cent on big shells and 60 per cent on 18-pounders and hence the fact that the British offensive no longer overtakes the output of shells, but, on the contrary, the close of each phase of the offensive, as at Messines, finds the reserve of shells bigger than at the start.

'Extension is illustrated by a shop which devotes itself almost exclusively to the mountings of howitzers. It is an entirely new construction of steel and glass, flimsy in appearance, but strong enough. It took only four months roughly to construct. Such are the results attained by utilising the very best gear-cutting machinery in the world and by the lifting of all peace-time restrictions.

'Alongside is the 12-in gun department, or rather the 12-in gun mounting department, for although this firm has a vast factory in another part of the country for actually manufacturing guns, only gun mountings are dealt with at Barrow. These are the guns which, buried solidly in the ground miles behind the fighting line, plough the German line with high explosives till it loses all shape and outline, and becomes only a long stretch of smoking hillocks and little valleys of fresh-turned earth. These guns proceed up country to the front on their own wheels, not so difficult a job or so devastating for the roads of France as it might be, for they trundle along in half-a-dozen parts, gun, cradle, carriage and so forth. When it reaches the front it takes something like seven hours to get this huge mass of metal solidly into the ground, but the actual mounting and dismounting can be a comparatively speedy process.

In general it may be said that the Barrow works are a striking manifestation of the extraordinary amount of technical skills, organising ability and enthusiasm which are being put into this side of the great work of rolling back the tide of Prussian militarism.

Perhaps the most striking thing to be seen here, as at the other munitions centres visited by the writer, is the keenness of these experts about their work. Experts are not always enthusiasts, but the directors and managers of Vickers certainly are. Their enthusiasm in all that pertains to the firm extends to the rare and privileged visitor, whose presence is treated as an honour, and who finds himself embarrassingly pursued wherever he goes by the firm's cinematographer, recording his every look of amazement or satisfaction.

Meantime, however, visitors are naturally infrequent. The close concentration of thought and energy by all concerned in the great problem of output forbids that. Rarely even do the heads of the firm take time to glance ahead at the problems of the use in peace time of the immense new buildings and the huge quantity of new plant, which have been set in Barrow by the urgent necessities of war.

German militarism is bending but is not yet broken and until that end is in sight Vickers Limited will concentrate solely on the winning of the war.

A Town Packed to Bursting

Under the headline of 'Labour unrest in Barrow' the Ulverston News *of 4 August 1917 outlined the grave problems of overcrowding facing an important munitions and war-work town which was bursting at the seams.*

The Industrial Unrest Commissioners for the north-west state in their report that on all occasions the witnesses prefaced their evidence by an expression of a desire to assist the government and their fellow citizens at the front to prosecute the war to a satisfactory conclusion.

Making the case of Barrow a special supplemental feature of their report, the commissioners say that the general propositions as to unrest are the same as in other portions of the area, but Barrow has its own special problems arising from its geographic isolation and the large influx of new population coming into the town to work at munitions. 'The wants of the citizens have undoubtedly been gravely neglected,' they say; and they found 'a most unsatisfactory condition of things existing' in relation to housing. For nearly three years the population of this important working centre has been constantly increasing; and there was no evidence that either the government or the municipality had taken any practical steps to deal with the problem that has been urgent all this time, and has now become a crying scandal.

It is a matter that the War Cabinet should at once hand over to some really authoritative person to deal with. What is wanted is someone entirely different in status and powers from the inspectors and other officials who have from time to time visited Barrow and made reports to London.

Someone might well be sent down without delay with a proper staff to formulate an emergency housing scheme and carry it out, with the full force of the Cabinet at his back, and with power to insist upon every department in London, including the Treasury, obeying his orders promptly. It is a bit of work for the war that wants doing – and wants doing at once.

The population of Barrow in 1911 was 64,594 and the number of houses 12,902. In 1917 the figures were 85,179 and 14,791

Many events were held to support several hundred Belgian refugees staying in Barrow during the First World War. The Great Belgian National Band gave a concert at Barrow's Palace Theatre in July 1915.

– and those statistics, the commissioners assert, are a terrible indictment against the rulers and governors, whoever they may be, who are responsible for providing homes for the workers, many of whom are legally prevented from leaving their employment without the permission of a tribunal.

At the outbreak of war there was a well-recognised shortage of houses in Barrow, and this was, or ought to have been, understood by the authorities. 'At all events it did not take Vickers three years to discover that there would be such a thing as a housing problem in Barrow,' the commissioners say, in praising the firm for the steps it had taken to provide housing. Describing the conditions of overcrowding which prevail, one witness told the commissioners that 'The number of beds occupied by night and day on the box and cox principle is very high and runs into thousands.'

The same witness pointed to 'the very inadequate provision for maternity cases. In many houses it is impossible to deal with them, at any rate, with decency. Cases have been brought to my notice where nine persons have lived in one room, sixteen in one small house; and a bedroom is occupied by two grown-up sisters and their two brothers, sixteen and seventeen years of age.'

The exorbitant charges for lodgings, the 'cornering' of food rendered easy by Barrow's isolated situation, and the beer question are among other causes of local unrest.

Food Cornering Hits Barrow

Shortage of housing was not the only problem to affect the greatly increased wartime population of Barrow. Certain types of food, particularly beer, were often hard to find, as local producers and retailers could be tempted to ration unofficially sought-after items to their favoured customers. Food cornering was the name given to this activity and the Ulverston News *of 4 August 1917 was keen to stamp it out.*

This the Food Controller should stop at once; and owing to the peculiar position of the locality it should be as easy for him to corner the supplies as it seems to have been to those who in time of war have placed their own interests before those of the state.

There were complaints that the amount of beer coming into Barrow is the same now or less than it was prior to the war; and that the public houses are apparently closed to the public, but that favourite customers can obtain entrance by the back door, and consume not only their own share, but more than is good for them.

The result of all this is to drive such men as are in receipt of good wages to buy bottles of spirits, take them home and consume them too rapidly. This evil, it is said, is also spreading among women. In the present crowded state of the houses, if this be true, it is a tragic picture, and the remedy for it is to reopen the public houses, consider carefully local needs in settling the hours of opening and supply an honest beer at a fair price to all well-conducted clubs and public houses.

Men who are living under the conditions we have described, some young and thoughtless, others young and thoughtful, and all undoubtedly infected by a spirit of revolt that is not altogether unnatural, are inspired by a feeling that the government so far away from them are not taking any human interest in their affairs.

They therefore attempt to remedy their grievances and bring about a better condition of things by calling attention to their wrongs using methods of stoppages and strikes which interfere with the output of munitions, but which in their lack of knowledge they consider is the only language that reaches Whitehall.

The taking away of the right to strike

The Co-operative Society store on Powerful Street, Vickerstown – a street whose name has shipbuilding connections. Many shops found it difficult to get supplies during the First World War.

This Red Cross ambulance designed to carry eight wounded soldiers during the First World War was paid for by fund-raising events held at Barrow schools.

has greatly destroyed the influence of trade unions and thrown the power into the hands of irresponsible people who make the most of the unhappy conditions of the town to press forward very extreme views of social and political reconstruction which we do not think they themselves fully understand, and which we are sure have at present no great hold upon the loyal and law-abiding community of Barrow.

Barrow Demands 1,000 Houses

Such was the shortage of places to live in Barrow for munitions workers that the Board of Guardians called on the Ministry of Munitions to build 1,000 houses immediately. To press the matter, a series of 'typical cases' was described to show how bad the overcrowding was in many town streets. A newly opened house bureau had records of 600 cases of chronic overcrowding. Famine prices were in operation with many single rooms being sub-let for more than the rent on the entire house. A report in the Ulverston News *of 1 September 1917 outlined the problems faced by workers.*

A father and mother and four children (one over sixteen years of age) sleep in the same bedroom. They live in a damp and dimly lighted cellar in the daytime. For this accommodation (unfurnished) they pay 7s a week. The mother told me they have lived in this fashion for three years. A second room in the same house is let for 6s, unfurnished.

'In another house thirteen persons, old and young, occupy two small bedrooms. There are houses in which each of the four rooms is tenanted by a separate family. Eight families live in a house of a larger type in Duke Street. It is not uncommon to find sixteen and seventeen persons living in four rooms.

A man gave me the following details of the place in which he lives. A woman and six children sleep in a back room, another woman and four children in the middle room, a lodger has a third room, a woman and three children have the parlour, the old landlady sleeps on the sofa in the kitchen and he and his family have the remaining room.

There is a six-roomed house (two living rooms, two bedrooms, two attics) that has nineteen occupants, including a family of nine, six of whom are over sixteen years of age. A man, his wife and three children live in the kitchen in a two-roomed house in Ship Street and five persons occupy the other room, which can only be reached through the kitchen. In Latona Street six men lodgers sleep in a room which three beds fill so completely that there is nowhere to put their personal belongings, except beneath their beds.

Too Little, Too Late

The frequent complaints from Barrow about overcrowding finally had an effect. In September 1917 Winston Churchill at the Ministry of Munitions agreed to meet a delegation from the town and finally accepted that the government had a duty to house at least some of the thousands of new workers it was forcing to move to Barrow.

In October the Ministry of Munitions accepted the need to build 500 permanent and 500 semi-permanent houses in Barrow. It took a year to do anything more – except argue over who would set the rents and how many rooms the different types of houses would have.

The original government scheme for 400 houses at Abbotsmead on land between Risedale Road and Salthouse Lane was gradually cut back in scale to 250. They were built by Barrow Corporation and the work continued despite the war ending and the munitions workers going home. The original overcrowding problem may have gone but there was still a general government policy to increase the housing stock to counter social and industrial unrest. It was December 1920 before all the houses were completed. They included houses at Monks Brow, Friars Lane, Priors Path, Holcroft Hill, Abbots Vale and Walton Lane.

For Those who Never Returned

The First World War ended on 11 November 1918 but the town waited three years to get its formal opportunity to mark the loss of life with the unveiling of the Barrow Park war memorial. Most families in Barrow had lost someone in the fighting – or least knew or went to school with a soldier who would never be coming back. Appropriately, the unveiling ceremony was held on Armistice Day and thousands turned out to watch. The *North-Western Daily Mail*'s editorial said: 'It was one of the saddest and yet one of the proudest days in the history of Barrow.' The paper called for action to remember the casualties of war – the killed, the grieving and the war survivors who now struggled to find work in a town gripped by recession. 'It is only by discharging fully our obligations to ex-servicemen and to the dependants of all who fought for us that we can hope to square our account with those who gave their lives for us and ours,' said the paper.

Barrow mayor Walker Fairbairn said: 'If today we can realize that the spirit of collective effort, good will and fortitude is bound eventually to win through, Armistice

The unveiling ceremony for the war memorial in Barrow Park on 11 November 1921.

Alderman Walker Fairbairn was Barrow's Mayor when the memorial was unveiled. He called on the town to support those who had suffered in the four-year conflict.

Field Marshal Sir William Robertson who officially unveiled Barrow War Memorial.

Day 1921 may prove the opening of a brighter era, and we shall be the more worthy of the blood-bought heritage secured to use by the men whose memory is so vividly before us today.'

The cenotaph was unveiled by Field Marshal Sir William Robertson. The newspaper reported: 'The sounding of a buzzer and the boom of a field gun announced that the fateful hour on which the Armistice was declared – 11am – had arrived. Sir William Robertson at once pressed a lever which cut a cord attached to two huge Union Flags folded over the memorial and in an instant the flags dropped and there was presented to the gaze of the multitude the massive structure scintillating in the brilliant sunshine.'

The Bishop of Carlisle told the crowds: 'They died, it was true, to save England and no one has any right to belittle in any way the magnitude of their achievements. No one can express how great and how far-reaching might prove to be the victory which they helped to win and what they did would be written large in the future history of the world.'

Counting the Cost of War

The Infield convalescent home was a practical part of Barrow's tribute to the sacrifices made during the First World War. However, the funding to keep it in good order was as dependent on the prosperity of the town as everything else and so the home suffered in the trade recession which started soon after the Armistice. Its gardens were allowed to grow wild prompting a Barrow News *reader to call for action on 16 September 1922:*

What has gone wrong with the Infield Convalescent Committee? The grounds are in a shocking state, paths grown over with weeds and moss, valuable rose trees and shrubs growing wild and going to ruin and waste. Could nothing be done at once to prevent waste which will cost fabulous money whenever the place is required for use? There are plenty of men between fifty and sixty years of age who know this work from experience and one or two men would make a big difference to the paths, terrace and shrubs in a month.

If the committee are so poor that they cannot afford to spend some of the revenue from the house, grounds and lodge, they might go round and canvass for one shilling per week subscribers (I will be one) to pay for some help, and the park gardener, if given the liberty, could visit the place once a day and give instruction. There is not a day to be lost if ruin is to be prevented.

Barrow marked the sacrifice of the First World War in many ways, including this convalescent home at Infield.

The War Memorial Convalescent Home was demolished in April 1968 to make way for housing. It had been built in the 1870s and owners included Vickers and a Barrow mayor, T.F. Butler.

Giant Relic of the Great War

Biggar Bank on Walney still offers sun, sea and sand to visitors but among its more unusual attractions used to be a First World War tank. Its curious lozenge shape stood pointing skywards on a pile of rocks on a site now occupied by the Roundhouse. The tanks were handed out as a reward for work towards the war effort. Similar machines of war once stood at Tank Square in Ulverston and in Millom Park. Barrow's tank arrived at Barrow railway station on 26 February in 1920 and lumbered its way to Walney at walking pace. Its dramatic arrival was reported by the North-Western Daily Mail *under the heading 'Local war trophy for Biggar Bank':*

The tank which has been presented to the town of Barrow for financial assistance accorded during the war set out today for the site prepared for it at Biggar Bank, Walney. Under command of Lt Hepworth, this instrument of war, weighing 30 tons, moved out of the Furness Railway goods yard about 11.20 a.m. but before it had got clear of the gates some valve trouble was experienced and a halt had to be made until the machinery was righted. After about half-an-hour's delay the engine again began to throb and the tank crawled out into the roadway, snorting and grunting, and emitting petrol fumes.

Some apprehension was felt as to whether she could safely negotiate the Low Level Bridge separating Devonshire Dock from the Devonshire Basin, but it was decided to take the risk and the bridge was crossed without mishap. A considerable crowd assembled to see the tank, which will no doubt be an object of interest and curiosity to the thousands of visitors to Biggar Bank now and in years to come.

She is of an early type, belonging to the K group, her top speed being from two to three miles an hour on a good surface, and she consumes from four to five gallons of petrol per mile. This is the first war trophy to be given to Barrow, and it is rather appropriate that it should have taken the form of a tank, because this is one of the very few war products in the manufacture or invention of which Barrow claims no part.

After crossing the Low Level Bridge the tank again came to a standstill, but later in the day it was able to proceed on its journey.

The tank stood guard over the island until 1928 when councillors, keen to sweep away relics of conflict, voted to be rid of it. The council minutes of 7 May that year recorded:

It was moved by Alderman Longstaffe, and seconded by Alderman Morton, that the time has now come for the fostering in every direction of the spirit of peace between the nations and towards this end it is necessary to create the peace 'outlook' among the younger generation, as the surest guarantee of peace in the future.

As a gesture of the genuineness of the desire for peace as expressed in our many utterances, we hereby resolve that all relics of the late war at present exhibited in our schools, and on Biggar Bank, be collected and sold to the highest bidder, and the proceeds of such sale be allocated to the funds of the Tuberculosis After-Care Committee, to be used by such committee to help repair some of the damage created by the mad adventure of 1914-1918.

The First World War tank presented to Barrow can be clearly seen in the centre of this picture of West Shore in the 1920s.

CHAPTER 6
Recession Bites

A summer scene with the shop sun blinds down on Dalton Road in the late 1920s or early 1930s. Times were hard in Barrow with few families having cash for luxuries.

Hard Times for Barrow

For those who still had jobs, the years after the First World War were ones of industrial unrest – often punctuated with pay disputes and strike action. One example was the wages grievance which brought Barrow port to a standstill in February 1920. The North-Western Daily Mail *of 18 February reported:*

Four hundred Barrow members of the Dock, Wharf, Riverside and General Workers' Union are out on strike and the port machinery is at a standstill. The discharge of a number of vessels, including timber, cement and ore boats, has been

The entire town suffered in the trade recession. Here the top of a Vickers crane provides an aerial vantage point.

delayed in consequence of the dispute and it may be that if an early settlement is not forthcoming local shipping activities will become seriously interfered with.

The trouble has arisen, a *Mail* reporter was informed by one of the men's representatives, over wages in respect of the unloading of manganese ore. Even before the war, apparently, it had been the custom in Barrow to pay the men an extra penny an hour in respect of the work among manganese ore because of the heaviness of the labour and certain dangers to health which it involved. Today, or rather last week, the rate of pay in operation was 1s 8½d per hour for general cargoes with an extra penny per hour for cargoes of manganese ore.

Last week a vessel, the *War Turn*, arrived with 6,000 tons of manganese ore and on Thursday the men engaged discharging the consignment urged one of their colleagues to ask for a greater concession than the extra penny, which they considered was inadequate for the work. He was given a mandate by them to ask for at least 2s per hour. No concession, however, could be gained through the parley which the men's nominee had with representatives of the Furness Railway Company on Thursday and Friday and on Saturday morning the men refused to work.

In sympathy with the manganese ore workers, other dock labourers have ceased work and today the life of the docks was totally suspended. Yesterday, Mr Cusack of Workington, the district secretary and organizer of the union, visited Barrow and interviewed representatives of the railway company but apparently without any result satisfactory to the men.

A Year of Stagnation

The Barrow and District Year Book *for 1922 looked back in sorrow on a dire twelve months for the town.*

From the point of view of prosperity the town of Barrow during 1921 experienced a black year. The ranks of the unemployed were not fewer at any time in the twelve months than several thousands and the distress prevalent among the citizens generally was perhaps best illustrated by the fact that out-relief promised the Board of Guardians an overdraft at the bank of £15,000 by the end of January 1922.

The industries of the town were involved in the stagnation that enveloped the whole country. It is true that shipbuilding opened with promise, but in the later months it underwent a progressive decline until by the end of the year the outlook became exceedingly gloomy. Trade disputes, notably the joiners' strike, impeded progress on orders in hand and the general high cost of production not only occasioned the suspension of some commissions and the cancellation of others, but in addition precluded the possibility of new contracts being secured as succeeding vessels were launched.

In engineering, matters were not really busy, but at the time when the life of the shipbuilding trade seemed to be ebbing out, there were portents that suggested an early appreciable recovery in engineering employment.

Vickers secured the gun mountings for two of the super-Hood battle-cruisers and

An open-top electric tram, advertising the Coliseum picture house and Cooke's furniture store, just outpaces the walkers on Duke Street. The council took over the trams just as recession robbed them of fares from workers.

The building berths at the Vickers yard in Barrow. Orders were hard to find in the early 1920s.

the machinery for one, but following the opening of the Washington Conference on the limitation of armaments, the Admiralty suspended the construction of these capital ships. This suspension admittedly darkened the gloom and gave a set-back to other possible contracts.

At the iron and steel works complete stagnation was the order for much the greater portion of the year. Even when at last in the autumn a restart was made at some of the blast furnaces the remunerative production of iron was scarcely possible. Business was very feeble and pending modifications in fuel and working costs pointed to the fact that 1922 would be well in before the slump could be described as finally left behind.

Disorderly Scenes at Barrow

The town came close to civil war in May 1922 as shipyard workers were split over accepting the company terms to settle an overtime dispute which had led to a lock-out of the engineers. The company claimed that half of those involved had accepted an offer to return to work – on individual contracts. They faced angry crowds, pickets and abuse. The house of one worker was scrawled with 'scab' and 'blackleg'. The local newspapers were packed with reports on different aspects of the dispute – but it was the growing resentment which dominated the headlines. In one report from the Barrow News *violence had broken out on Walney Promenade.*

The industrial dispute has produced its first scene of violence in Barrow. A crowd variously estimated at between 300 and 500 strong, in which women predominated, gathered on the Promenade to wait for the return home of such residents from the island as had gone into work. Whether there were other such men living on the island or not, at least two came under the attention of the waiting assembly and neither escaped without personal injury. Had it not been for the presence of the police, who had to go to their rescue, their experience might have been much worse than it was. Even with the intervention of policemen, one of them could not be removed out of danger until he had been almost brutally handled.

How Bad Can it Get?

In 1922 Barrow had sunk about as low as it could go. Thousands were without work and those still with jobs facing pressure to accept lower wages from firms close to going out of business. To make matters worse, government rules on dole payments meant the unemployed faced eight weeks with no money. Under the heading '6,000 Barrow men's dole to stop' the Barrow News of 9 September 1922 painted a grim picture:

Something in the nature of a bombshell was dropped by a representative of the Barrow Employment Exchange at a meeting of the Work for the Unemployed sub-committee at Barrow when he made the announcement that persons, chiefly men, now drawing the dole would from the 19th and 20th September, have to go without the unemployment benefit for eight weeks until they again became entitled to this government palliative for unemployment.

This opens a very serious problem for the town. These men cannot live for eight weeks without food and food cannot be obtained without money and money cannot be earned without work and the Work for the Unemployed committee have not sufficient work coming forward to absorb a mere fraction of the men.

The result will probably be that the Board of Guardians will be inundated with further applications for relief at the expense of the ratepayers, and there are

Traders struggled on Dalton Road and elsewhere in Barrow as thousands survived on the dole.

Mikasa Street in 1907, part of Vickerstown and one of many streets named after Barrow-built ships. Without work, thousands of people struggled to pay their rents during the recession.

already about 11,000 on the relief list. At the present time there are only 158 men employed on relief work at Barrow and there are close on 16,000 altogether unemployed. It is impossible for the corporation to find work for all or even a big percentage.

Keeping the Landlord Happy

As thousands of families struggled to make ends meet it was often the house rent which went unpaid and what little cash was available went on food for the family and clothing for the children. Landlords saw their incomes dwindle and resorted to court action. The London Midland and Scottish Railway was owed a total of £10,000 by over 500 tenants in 1925. A report in the North-Western Daily Mail *of 17 June described the action taken.*

Applications for ejectments in respect of twenty-seven houses owned by the London Midland and Scottish Railway were dealt with at the Barrow Police Court this morning. Mr Hickson, who prosecuted on behalf of the LMS, explained the circumstances which had brought about the necessity for the applications in all the cases. He was instructed to make twenty-seven applications for ejectment orders for premises in Barrow owned by the company, known as the Barrow dwellings, which consisted of 568 flats, which were let in some cases at 6s 5d and in others 7s 8d per week. Arrears to the amount of over £10,400 was due to the company from the 568 tenants to 1 January 1925. Since January the arrears were, of course, much greater. During the course of the year the company had paid £4,184 in rates. As the magistrates were no doubt aware, continued Mr Hickson, the landlords were allowed to raise rents 40 per cent, in addition to which any increase in the rates could be put on to the rent.

The company had been very lenient,

however, and the rents had only been increased by 25 per cent, and the rates had not been added. The company had considered the matter for over 18 months and the arrears had accumulated; in several cases tenants had been sued in the county court for the rent owing. In the majority of cases orders had been made and as long as the rent was paid, plus a few pence in some cases, and as much as ten shillings in others, the orders had been suspended. Only fifteen cases had been taken up previous to that court and only two of the tenants had failed to comply with the order, which had, of course, been enforced.

The railway company had always acted reasonably and did not intend to be unreasonable in any case where the tenant was making an effort to pay. Sixty-seven cases had been sent down for hearing. Forty of those cases had been settled to the satisfaction of both owner and tenant. Of the twenty-seven cases which were down for hearing, one tenant had paid the arrears, amounting to £10 15s 8d in full and sixteen had offered to pay the current rent and 4d or 1s 4d off the arrears.

There were one or two bad cases, as much as £60 owing, and in others only £10. There were cases where general poverty was pleaded and he would ask for an order to be made and suspended. The cases were gone into and the bench made various orders asked for by the solicitor. The chairman of the bench, at the end of the hearing, congratulated Mr Hickson and the company on the lenient and most sympathetic way in which the tenants had been treated.

Looking down Dalton Road from Woolworth's around 1930.

The Jute Works at Hindpool was one of the victims of the recession in trade which hit Barrow soon after the end of the First World War.

Jute Factory Falls to Recession

One of the big casualties of the recession was the mighty Barrow Jute Works – although hopes were always held of an upturn in its fortunes. The North-Western Daily Mail *on Monday 11 May 1925 dared to hope that a buyer could be found for the empty factory.*

Considerable local interest is attached to the sale – or what is hoped will be a sale – this Wednesday when the extensive flax and jute works of the Barrow and Calcutta Company will be put up for public auction.

As is known, these works, which used to employ a large number of women and girls, have been closed for about three years, and hopes are entertained that the premises will be purchased by some firm which will lose no time in getting the wheels of industry going again. It would be a great boon to Barrow, particularly just now, to have this factory in full activity once more.

When it closed down, what had been for many years one of the chief sources of employment for female labour was removed. What the future has in store for the works remains to be seen. The proceedings on Wednesday may mark the beginning of a new industrial development in the town.

Such commodious and substantial premises, with the excellent machinery and equipment, should not be allowed to remain idle. The Jute Mills were commenced in 1870 by a limited liability company, of which the then Duke of Devonshire was chairman. The object then, as it should be today, was to provide work for young women. In 1879 a fire occurred, which destroyed a large portion of the building, and this was never rebuilt. This disastrous fire limited the number of workpeople to about half the original number. A second destructive fire took place in 1891. From 1897 the works, after being reconstructed and brought up to date, were owned by the Barrow and Calcutta Jute Company Limited, whose head offices were in Liverpool, but the property changed hands a few years ago.

The works occupy about 12 acres with frontages to Hindpool Road, Ramsden Square, Abbey Road, Duke Street and Clive Street, and have a private siding to the railway. The original directors, being anxious to secure as far as possible the cleanliness and cheerfulness of the workers, had the walls lined several feet high with light glazed bricks, having an ornamental border, and divided into compartments by tiles, bearing the monogram and trade mark of the company. The materials used in the construction of the buildings are excellent red bricks made in the locality, interspersed with terracotta and Yorkshire stone for dressings. The style of architecture is an adaptation of Italian. The principal façade faces Hindpool Road and overlooks the docks, the centre feature being a large block of buildings containing general offices, board room, store rooms, mess rooms, lodge, principal entrance etc. There is a large courtyard, with engine houses and a large workshop, with all modern appliances for engineering, smith work and millwright work.

The works have been engaged in the spinning of jute yarn, and in the manufacture of jute goods, including bags for sugar, flour, grain, coffee, wool, cotton, chemicals etc, also fabrics for linoleum, floor cloth, packing and general purposes. The raw jute was imported in bales from Calcutta and stored in the company's warehouses and in the jute warehouses at Devonshire Dock. In the spinning sheds it passed through various machines

Celebrating the harvest festival at the Barrow Sailors' Rest in 1922. Few would have been able to donate produce in what was a dire year for the town.

The tall chimneys of Barrow ironworks were a dominant feature on the skyline. In 1921 work was at a standstill as the owners searched for orders in a depressed market.

for softening, carding, drawing, roving, spinning, spool and cop winding.

The yarns then passed into the beaming sheds and then to the weaving departments, where they were made into fabrics of various weights, texture and widths. After leaving the weaving sheds, the cloth passed through the inspecting room, where it was measured, weighed and examined. It then went to the cloth finishing department, when it was cropped, calendered, mangled, lapped, or put into large rolls, or press packed into bales for shipment or for home consumption.

'The fabrics for bag-making were drawn up into the floors above by the cutting machines, which, at the same time, cut them into the various lengths required; they later were sewn by sewing machinery into sacks and bags, with tarred or dry twine. The bags were then marked by printing machinery, after which they were folded and made up into bundles.

False Dawn at Shipyard

On 16 April 1925 the North-Western Daily Mail *reported signs of optimism from Barrow shipyard, despite big financial losses.*

Speaking at the fifty-eighth annual meeting of Vickers Limited at Sheffield, Mr Douglas Vickers (the chairman) said Barrow, unfortunately, had made a considerable loss, mainly due to the completion of certain ships and engineering orders for which the company contracted in 1923, which they deliberately tendered on labour and materials with only part charges and without profit in order to keep the yard at work and avoid the still greater loss that would have followed closing down.

Conditions had improved a little there, and the number of men employed had risen gradually to nearly 10,000 as compared to 5,000 in 1923. They had finished a Cunarder, and they had under construction for the Orient Company a sister ship to the *Orama*. They had also under construction one of the new cruisers, as well as a fair amount of ordnance work in connection with ships building in government dockyards.

The company had also been informed that they were to receive a valuable order from the Australian government in connection with their naval programme. As with 10,000 men employed they were getting near the point when normal charges were absorbed, the prospects for 1925 at Barrow seemed better. On the other hand there were no inquiries at present for cruisers or large liners – the work that suited the yard best – and the outlook for the latter half of next year was not good at present.

Everybody Out on Strike

The hard times of the 1920s had many low points in Barrow as long-established firms made men and women redundant or failed altogether. It was a mirror of events in countless other industrial towns and those frustrations made themselves felt in a dramatic way during 1926 in the General Strike. It had started over coal but rapidly took on a political dimension and affected many industries throughout the country. The Evening Mail reported in great detail the announcement of the strike for 4 May, and the text of the emergency declared by King George V. As an employer the newspaper opposed the strike and published for

Specialist staff at Vickers who worked with engineering moulds and marked off metal plates for cutting, September 1935. The picture was taken near the end of the shell shop. By this time the good days were returning.

the last time on Monday 3 May, with a story saying 'Strike order must be withdrawn.' It was to be the last paper published for a fortnight. The strike stopped the trams, buses and trains. Coal had to be rationed for home use and shops faced shortages as most goods in 1926 were moved by rail. When the Evening Mail published again on 14 May it described the events of the strike in Barrow.

It would be idle of course, to suggest that the effects of the General Strike did not penetrate into this corner of England, but all essential services were fully maintained. One of the most deplorable features of the strike locally has been its detrimental effect on industry. The iron and steelworks were obliged to close down at the beginning of the week owing to the lack of fuel supplies, and thus thousands of men in Furness and Cumberland were thrown idle.

Before the end of the first week these important industries which so vitally affect Barrow and the surrounding districts were completely paralysed and it is difficult to say how far-reaching may be the consequences.

The paper waited until 17 May to deliver its own editorial verdict on the strike.

Good hearts and clear heads broke the General Strike – the attempt of the Trades Union Congress to blackmail the nation. There are some of the men's leaders who are trying to make themselves as well as other people believe, that the General Strike was called off because they had achieved what they wanted – that the miners would have justice. What rubbish. The nation, as a whole, has never been against the miners; there is sympathy for the coal-getters, and

Times were hard after the First World War and Barrow's unemployment problems were taken direct to the government as part of a national march to London.

Massive gun turntables under construction in the gun mounting department at Vickers-Maxim. A cancelled order for these in 1921 was a major blow to recession-hit Barrow.

the hazards of their occupation call for consideration. But the General Strike failed because the people backing the government determined that they would not be dictated to or brow-beaten by a small group of men who represented a minority in the country and who had gulled themselves that they were above the law and Parliament.

CHAPTER 7
Transport

The Stone Trough on Abbey Road was the traditional boundary of Barrow. This photograph of a bowler-hatted cyclist dates from around 1890.

The Tram Comes to Barrow

The first mention of public road transport in the new and rapidly expanding town was back in 1877 when two horse buses began to take passengers from the Ship Inn on Barrow Island, through the town centre and along Abbey Road to the Strawberry Hotel. In 1883 a special Barrow committee visited tramways throughout the north of England and recommended a four-foot gauge tram system for the town.

It took until 11 July 1885 for the track to be laid and the first services started. William Parsons drove the first tram and the system operated with eight trams from a depot in Salthouse Road. A year later, with the High Level Bridge completed, the tram system extended to Ramsden Dock. By Queen Victoria's Diamond Jubilee in 1897 there were six miles of tram track in Barrow, but a year later the tram company was bankrupt.

It was bought by the British Electric Traction Company in 1899 and by 1903

Waiting for an electric tram outside the Conservative Club on Abbey Road in 1905.

steam trams had stopped, ready for electrification. In February 1904 the first electric trams ran and by 1909 the system had reached Walney Promenade at Ferry Road. By 1911 the system was at its greatest extent with trams to Biggar Bank.

At the end of the First World War Barrow Corporation bought the tram system but as recession hit Furness, and unemployed workmen no longer needed to get to the shipyard in huge numbers, the trams proved to be a major drain on the rates.

It all came to an end on 5 April 1932 when the last three trams ran from Abbey terminus. One of the drivers was the same William Parsons who took control of Barrow's first tram nearly fifty years earlier.

The redundant tram system had thirty-one trams in stock and until at least the early 1970s some of them were in use as holiday huts on the Coast Road to Ulverston. Buses replaced the trams and in 1936 a new transport depot was opened in Hindpool Road, costing £20,360.

During a heavy Second World War air raid in 1941 buses were used to transport women and children to the countryside.

Driver Becomes a Local Celebrity

Barrow's first tram driver had become a local celebrity long before the closing of the system. In the North-Western Daily Mail *of 31 January 1920 he was given star treatment with a detailed profile on 'The oldest Barrow tram employee'.*

When Barrow Corporation took over the tramway undertaking of the British Electric Traction Company on New Year's Day, there also entered into the employ Motorman

An electric tram outside the Majestic Hotel on Duke Street in 1929.

William H. Parsons, who is not only the oldest tramway servant in the borough, but the only one of the employees who was so engaged when the first tram service – the old steam cars – began running in 1885.

Mr Parsons is not by birth a Barrovian, though by residence he can qualify as such, for he came here from his native Warwickshire – he was born near Birmingham – in 1874, and a residence of forty-six years should entitle him to be called a Barrovian. He was a boy of twelve when he came to the town, and his first place of employment was at the steelworks.

His connection with the tram service began in a curious manner. He was asked to lend a hand in getting the engines up. These were from Messrs Kitson of Leeds. He did this and he also borrowed coal from the Vulcan works to get up steam on the first engine.

Mr Parsons seems to have done his work satisfactorily and when the first manager – Mr Wilkinson – came to the town, Mr Parsons went to meet him and take him down to the depot. It was not long before the manager asked him to throw in his lot with the service and he has been in it ever since.

He drove the first steam car in 1885 to pass the inspection of Major Hutchinson, of the Board of Trade. 'On that car were Sir James Ramsden, Councillors Morgan and Whittam and other councillors who I cannot remember now,' said Mr Parsons in an interview, 'but I do know that the only two who rode on that car who are now living are Mr S. Lord JP and myself. The Lord and the Parson remain.'

Continuing, Mr Parsons said: 'I drove in the last car of the old steam trams. I remember it well, because just as I was leaving, I was called back because a fire had broken out at the depot and I helped to extinguish it. But the cars were not altogether stopped even then. The manager was besieged with requests for a service, even if it was only one car per hour. An hour service was subsequently put on, and the cars ran thus until the engines were finally condemned. I remember this because I was helping Mr Dudley Wright at this time against Councillor Mawson and as I was passing the depot the manager called me, explained what the public wanted and asked if I would help. I consented and ran the hour service till it was abolished. I commenced with the electric service in 1904 and am now with the corporation. I have been under six managers – Messrs Wilkinson, McClay, Burgoyne, Bladon, Dobson and Groves, the present head.'

Mr Parsons wears four gold stripes and they have, as to three of them, been awarded in each case successively for two years' good conduct and no accidents. As to the fourth, an exciting story is to be told.

One night in 1915, Mr Parsons was on a car coming from Roose in the direction of the town, when a car came out of the depot on the wrong line of rails and made straight for the oncoming car. After shouting and using the bell, it was seen that no one was on the other car. Mr Parsons had his car reverse, jumped off, ran forward, got on to the runaway and succeeded in pulling it up within a very short distance of his own car. It was an exciting moment, and a dangerous situation was saved by the promptitude of Mr Parsons. For this he received the personal thanks of the local manager, a similar letter of thanks from the directors, a gift of £3 3s and the additional gold stripe.

Mr Parsons has now been on tram service in the town for the long period of thirty-five years and looks healthy and strong enough for many years more of such splendid service as he has already rendered to the borough.

Never a Tram When you Need it

Late trains, dirty buses: it is human nature to complain at the level of service on public transport. Back in 1920 it was the trams which took the flak – particularly as the Barrow Corporation had just taken them over. In the North-Western Daily Mail *on 16 March the paper made sure the town hall knew there was still room for improvement.*

Now that the tramcars are the property of the town, it is to be hoped there will soon be an improved service and that as far as possible the time-table will be strictly adhered to. At present would-be passengers are obliged to take their chance, but it must be admitted that a better service has been introduced since the undertaking changed hands.

When the ten new cars are available, then the townspeople may look for a still quicker service and incidentally the corporation should be able to rake in the shekels more abundantly in the shape of fares, for more people now walk rather than wait for an overcrowded car; and when the rain raineth, upper decks provide no shelter.

Complaint has been received in regard to Walney cars turning at the Promenade after passengers had booked for Amphitrite Street. On inquiries a *Mail* reporter was informed that this is never done, or should not be done, unless a car is late and is followed immediately by another car proceeding to Amphitrite Street, to which passengers may be transferred. Delays on the Walney route are unfortunately inevitable, as the cars are occasionally held up through the High Level

The opening of the High Level Bridge in Barrow during 1908. Spectators stand on the tram lines as dignitaries pass by in a coach and horses.

Bridge being up. However, as far as possible the convenience of passengers should be studied and they should not be compelled to dismount until they have reached their destination unless another car is waiting for their reception. This is the regulation. An inspector, however, may use his discretion in sending back one car at the Promenade, or for that matter at any point of the route, if he finds, as we have often seen in Barrow, two cars bound for the same place and both half-empty.

Still it should not be possible, especially on those routes on which there are no bridges to cross, for two trams to be running one behind the other, except when the workmen are swarming home for dinner or tea.

At the present time a car is run to Biggar Bank every hour, but at Easter this service will be augmented to cope with the crowds desirous of visiting the popular rendezvous, and later on the summer service of $7\frac{1}{2}$ minutes will be re-established.

One Man and his Horse

Before the widespread use of commercial vans and wagons delivery of goods from port or rail station to shop and from shop to home often relied on the horse and cart. The photograph on page 103 is from the collection of Barrovian Brian Edge, who now lives near Crewe. Mr Edge said: 'The horse is Tommy and he is shown with Johnnie Jackson, who was a parcel van driver at Barrow Central station from the 1940s to the mid-1950s. Johnnie is shown wearing clogs and in the uniform of the London Midland and Scottish Railway. Tommy was always smartly turned out and he pulled a covered wagon, delivering parcels from the station to shops in Dalton Road, mainly

Woolworth traffic. His favourite titbit was reached by straying onto the pavement outside Dales greengrocers and eating the steaming beetroot that was freshly boiled and displayed in a basket in the doorway of the shop. Tommy was eventually retired and spent the last years of his life in a field at Broughton.

Driving Before the Jams

We are used to seeing cars and wagons everywhere but in 1936 the era of motoring for all was still a long way off. Figures presented by the Barrow News *on 21 March showed just how few vehicles were then on the road.*

From returns recently issued by the Ministry of Transport it appears that 220 new cars were registered during the year which ended September, 1935, an increase of 37 on the previous year. The 60 new goods delivery vehicles were five down on the preceding year.

The total number of vehicles registered during the same period was: cars, 1,210, against 1,042; goods delivery vehicles, 290, as compared with 252; and motor-buses, coaches and other hackney vehicles 73, against 70. These totals show an increase of 209 vehicles registered – or 15.3 per cent.

These figures show that there was a very satisfactory increase in the number of new motor vehicles sold and registered for the first time in Barrow during the

Heavy horse Tommy shown with Johnnie Jackson, who was a parcel van driver at Barrow railway station from the 1940s to the mid-1950s.

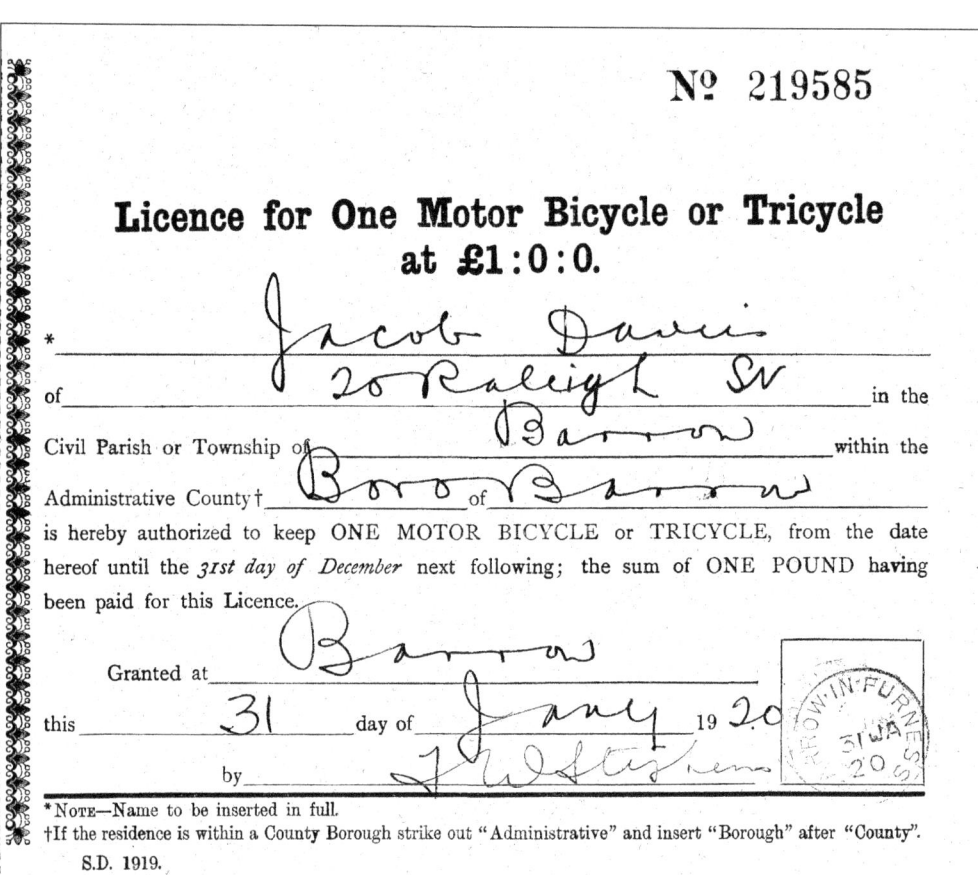

An early motorcycle licence issued to Jacob Davies in 1920.

year, as compared with 1934. And although there was an advance of 209 in the total registrations in the borough, no fewer than 73 old automobiles bearing the Barrow mark were placed out of commission during the twelve months and not re-licensed.

Coppernob *Draws the Crowds*

Barrow's first and most famous steam locomotive – Coppernob – has always been something of a celebrity. After its long service with the Furness Railway ended in 1899 it found a dignified retirement in a huge glass and iron case at the side of the old Barrow Central station. A Second World War bombing raid destroyed the ornate case and left the ageing locomotive's brass and copperwork with a few war wounds. It is now a star attraction at the National Railway Museum in York but as early as 1925 was drawing the crowds at another major venue. The North-Western Daily Mail of 6 June 1925 described the scene at a great exhibition being held at the new Wembley stadium in London.

Mr William Wignall, *Coppernob*'s old driver, who has just returned to Barrow from a visit to Wembley, where he has been to see his old companion of the metals, cannot find words to express his wonder at the great exhibition. 'No one,' he said to our representative today, emphasising his statement with a tap of his stick, 'should miss seeing Wembley, it is just too wonderful to describe.'

Mr Wignall said he felt very reminiscent when he saw the old copper-domed engine resting in the shade of a huge leviathan of the rails and even the laughter and noise of the large crowd pouring past could not stay the flood of memory. 'I was a little bit amazed at the big crowd round *Coppernob*,' he added naively, and he was interested to hear their comments on the engine. To many it seemed a strange sight after the modern locomotive but one or two hit the mark when they described it as a link between the old *Puffing Billy* and the present day. Under the guidance of Mr Phillips, of the London Midland and Scottish Railway, Mr Wignall later enjoyed a tour of the exhibition.

This chanced to be his first visit to London also, and when asked how he liked the Empire capital, said although he did not see very much of the city he was altogether delighted with his stay there, and intends to go again if he is spared. 'It's a mighty busy place,' was his comment, 'but no one should miss going there and seeing Wembley and dear old *Coppernob*.'

Waiting Too Long for a Bridge

The editorial column of the Vickerstown Chronicle *of 6 May 1904 argued a strong case for a road bridge linking the Barrow mainland to Walney.*

It is often asserted by superficial students of our insular habits that we are a militant people in Vickerstown. The charge is groundless. True, we have had to assert our rights and have to beat back the forces of

The venerable steam locomotive Coppernob *worked on the Furness Railway until 1899 and can now be seen at the National Railway Museum in York.*

The Walney Ferry is packed with travellers and ready to move off for the mainland in 1905.

prejudice and ill will which surrounded the creation of our homes. Now that is gone, and there is only one thing material which remains for us to strenuously fight for, and that thing is our long looked-for bridge.

When that is settled for ever in our favour, we shall turn our whole attention to peaceful vocations. The latest report says that the Bridge Bill will not be gone into by the House of Commons until after Whitsuntide. This is most disappointing, as we had hoped to have our rejoicings during the holidays. But in the meantime it is rumoured, and we think, with some semblance of truth, that the corporation and the only opponents to the popular bridge – the Furness Railway Company – are in touch with each other with, it is understood, the object of endeavouring to patch up the matter and thus save the town and the shareholders of the railway company the further expenditure of money in law, which is urgently needed in many other directions.

Whether we are dubbed militant or not, we rejoice in the news. The case for the bridge is so irrefutably convincing, and the shipping requirements of this neglected portion of the channel so microscopic, that, after the emphatic decision of the House of Lords, we feel that the railway company would be ill advised in pursuing the matter in the lower house. The final result would just be the same, and the cost of securing the confirmatory verdict would be enormous by going the House of Commons with their opposition, probably the opponents would put themselves completely at the mercy of the town, and any question of compensation for the ferry which may presently occupy the minds of the council would suddenly depart when the law costs of the second fight came to be considered.

An artist's impression from 1906 showing how the completed Walney Bridge would look.

One of Barrow's lost railway halts – the Furness Abbey station – on a postcard from around 1905.

An impressive commercial stand taken by the Furness Railway Company designed to attract visitors to the Lake District during the Franco-British Exhibition held in London in 1908.

The general feeling on the rumoured compromise is favourable, though not a few enthusiasts wish a fight to the finish, in the interests, they think, of morality of local public affairs. Too long, they say, Barrow has suffered from the tyranny of a railway company, and they welcome this as the day of at least partial deliverance. With this view we do not altogether agree. The Furness Railway Company has done much in the past for Barrow, through its Ducal magnates, and for that much Barrow's existence is an evergreen token of thankfulness. But the position of things has changed with years, and the Furness Railway Company has appreciably aged.

The railway company has the right to run the steam ferry across Walney Channel. The point is how much is that right worth? Linked with the right is an obligation created by agreement with certain landowners in Biggar and South End. To fulfil the terms of that agreement the ferry was installed, not, let it be noted, as a money-making concern. In due performance of this obligation the railway company ran the ferry for twenty years at a loss of, roughly, £800 a year. This was their alternative to paying a heavy claim for compensation. Assuming that they, with the astuteness which marked the early days of the railway directors, chose this as the less expensive of two courses, we find that the obligation of the railway company very materially discounts the goodwill of the ferry, which goodwill will be taken away by the erection of the bridge and transferred to the corporation with the costly obligation.

Who shall decide which way the balance goes? As regards the ferry itself, it has already run two years, and will run another two. It has been depreciated out of its own revenue at the rate of 5 per cent per annum, so that its four years' life would make it worth, roughly 20 per cent less than what it cost and probably it could fetch fully 50 per cent of its original value by a sale. As the old ferry ran for nearly twenty-five years it ought to have no book value. The case for a compromise is simple.

Rating Lane gets an Aerodrome

The First World War had given a great boost to the novelty of air flight. The aeroplanes developed to observe, and later to fight and bomb from high above the trenches, found new uses after 1918. The public had read about the flying aces of the war and wanted to see – and experience – this new method of travel. Flying shows were held all over the country and one Barrow business was not slow to see the financial opportunities. A Barrow cinema, the Salthouse Pavilion, took over part of Rating Lane in 1920 as a temporary aerodrome, booked a pair of planes from the Berkshire Aviation Company and made sure everyone knew about the event by placing advertisements in the local press. They proclaimed:

The management of the Salthouse Pavilion have arranged, at great expense, for a second aeroplane to come to Barrow to ensure that the numerous ladies and gentlemen who have booked flights for the weekend shall not be disappointed.

Saturday afternoon and all day Sunday both machines will carry passengers. Special exhibition flying, looping, stunting and many marvellous new feats not yet seen in Barrow will be performed. Arrangements have been made with the Topical Film Company to take films of the passengers flying, also of the stunting and the spectators on the field. The exclusive rights to all these pictures for Barrow have been secured by

Barrow Central station, including the glass showcase which once housed the steam locomotive Coppernob, was a victim of the Barrow Blitz.

the Salthouse Pavilion and will be exhibited there next week.

The advertisements did the trick and dozens came forward to try out the thrills of air travel. The North-Western Daily Mail *of 26 February 1920 reported:*

The new sport of flying has caught on in Barrow. Up to last night over sixty passengers had been booked for the weekend, to say nothing of the others who will be anxious to pay their guinea on the field at Rating Lane. Flying will terminate on Sunday, and in order to avoid disappointment and at the same time secure a unique local film, the management of the Salthouse Pavilion have arranged, at considerable expense, for a second aeroplane to come to Barrow.

This machine will be piloted by an aviation officer who has had a large experience. Thus, on Saturday afternoon and all day on Sunday both machines will carry passengers, and visitors to the aerodrome are also promised a rare exhibition of aerial stunts never before witnessed in this part of the country.

Arrangements have also been made through the enterprise of the Salthouse Pavilion, in conjunction with the Topical Film Company, for an expert cinematograph operator to come over to Barrow at the weekend to take films of the passengers flying, of the thrilling feats in the air, of the spectators and surroundings, all of which should go towards the making of a very interesting moving picture. The exclusive rights of all these pictures for Barrow have been secured at the Salthouse cinema next week.

Yesterday the *Mail* intimated that a free flight would be given to any person in Barrow over eighty-two years of age. This was the age of the oldest passenger taken up at Carlisle, and Barrow has been given the opportunity of beating that record.

Mr James Spencer of 13 North Coats, Walney, thought he would have 'a shot at this,' and this morning he called at the *Mail* office to put forward his claim. Mr Spencer will be eighty-three on the 13th of next month. While Mr Spencer cannot claim seniority in years – though he may do in a month – over the Carlisle lady, his claim will be put before the Berkshire Aviation Company. Mrs Thomas, who has reached the advanced age of eighty-nine, is another applicant for a free flight. A native of Dalton, she now resides with Mr and Mrs E. Warriner at 156 Ramsden Street, Barrow. She is the grandmother of Percy Thomas, a member of the Barrow Northern Union rugby team. Mr Warriner, who came into the *Mail* office to put in the claim for Mrs Thomas, tells us that the old lady is very nimble and walked eleven miles the other day. She works like a Trojan and can thread a needle with anybody.

An Irishman, named James McMahon, of 13 Ramsden Dock Road, who will attain his eighty-fourth birthday on 4 April, is another applicant. He has been forty-three years in Barrow, having worked at the shipyard as a caulker for thirty-seven years.

Part of Rampside railway station survives as a private house. When this picture was taken in 1905 the route took passengers to Roa Island.

CHAPTER 8
Town Life

Costumed performers parade to the theme of 'Charity is Love' at a Barrow event held in 1908 at Cavendish Park.

Keep Healthy for a Penny a Week

Early healthcare in Barrow was rudimentary. In 1866 the Vicar of St George's, the Revd T.S. Barrett, provided a house for medical treatment which became known as St George's Hospital. Voluntary subscriptions provided the fittings and furniture but it could not cope with the rapid increase in industrial accidents and injuries as mining, ironworking and shipbuilding developed in the town.

A public meeting was held in the Old Town Hall in January 1870 and a steering group was formed with representatives from all the principal employers. Most of the workmen in the town contributed a penny a week – supplemented by cash from employers and charitable donations – to allow the hospital to expand. By 1875 a bigger hospital building was bought in School Street.

Barrow nurses, pictured in 1904 outside the old North Lonsdale Hospital.

Two years later work started on the new North Lonsdale Hospital on land opposite the existing School Street site. By 1898 the hospital had seven wards and a total of thirty-two beds, plus a dispensary, out patient rooms and operating theatre. The total cost of the building was £8,500.

Poor Left with Healthcare Crumbs

Today we take things like a free National Health Service for granted but before the Second World War access to medical services was directly related to your ability to pay. Those at the bottom of the pecking order in Barrow during the 1920s had to rely on the Poor Law Medical Service and the restricted access this granted to doctors. A letter from Mr J. Smith of Blake Street, published in the North-Western Daily Mail *of 27 April 1925, outlined the problems. He said:*

The sick poor of Barrow have just been supplied with medical cards which state that the surgery hours are from 9 to 9.30 a.m. and 5.30 p.m. to 6.30 p.m. The evening hours are, however, from 4 p.m. to 5 p.m., and no alteration is made on the cards to this effect. There is also no mention of the fact that on Thursdays and Sundays there are no surgery hours after morning in the case of Thursdays, and none at all on Sundays. Thus the sick poor have only allotted $8\frac{1}{2}$ hours per week when they may receive attention at the surgery.

Unfortunately, it does not stop there. On Tuesday last, a woman with two children stood from 5.30 p.m. for over one hour, and again on Thursday from 5.30 p.m. without seeing the doctor. On the latter date an old woman of seventy-nine years of age was standing for over one hour with little covering; also one of seventy-five years of age, in Paradise Street, in the bitter

Hospital staff at Barrow do their best to make Christmas happy for these youngsters in the 1930s.

cold, and without result too. On Thursday the number reached eight people and no surgery.

In the name of common sense, why were not the proper hours put on the cards before issue? Then again, in catering for the sick poor are the surgery hours sufficient? What about the notice board which was to be erected, and was passed by the previous board to be done? The sick poor have a right to the best and reasonable attention even if they are poor, and it is to be hoped that the present board will see that they get it.

Epidemics of Infectious Diseases

The early years of Barrow's industrial development threw thousands of people together in cramped and unsanitary conditions. The result was sporadic outbreaks of infectious diseases, often linked to poor quality water supplies. As the town matured and gained modern water supply and drainage facilities the epidemics grew less frequent – but there was always a reminder of their potency. In the Barrow News of 27 June 1936 the Barrow medical officer Dr T.A. Seekings explained the problems of a particularly bad year.

The year has been characterized by great prevalence of scarlet fever and diphtheria, which have run concurrently throughout the year. This prevalence was in full force for the first few months of the year, and as would be expected, waned during the summer months, only to increase again during the autumn.

Though never entirely absent, diphtheria has been sporadic in Barrow and for many years until 1934, during which year 263 cases were notified, and that year marks the beginning of the present epidemic wave. During 1935 a total of 359 cases were notified. It is extremely satisfactory to note that of these 359 cases only seven proved fatal, giving a case mortality of 1.92, compared with 5.9 per cent for England and Wales during 1934.

During the year there were 255 cases of scarlet fever notified. As accommodation at the Isolation Hospital was inadequate to meet the demands put upon it, cases of scarlet fever had to give way to the more serious disease, diphtheria.

Three deaths were recorded from whooping cough. During the year 438 cases were treated at the Infectious Diseases Hospital, Devonshire Road. The epidemic prevalence of diphtheria and scarlet fever made it quite impossible to admit nearly all the cases which should have been admitted, in spite of the fact that all possible space was utilized and the old wing brought into use again. Preference was given to cases of diphtheria, which is essentially a serious disease requiring skilled nursing, which as a rule can only be obtained in hospital.

The number of deaths from cancer totalled 93, equivalent to a death rate of 1.4 per thousand. Cases of tuberculosis notified were 128 in number.

Atmosphere of Quiet Comfort

The opening of the new North Lonsdale private nursing home, featuring the latest in modern design and technology, was reported in the Barrow News of 26 December 1936.

The new private nursing home opened on Saturday by Commander Sir Charles Craven RN OBE will fill a long-felt want in the town and will doubtless prove an important adjunct to the North Lonsdale Hospital. It is situated in Albert Street

North Lonsdale Hospital, around 1902.

and has direct communication both with the hospital and with the new nurses' staff quarters in Church Street.

The accommodation has been arranged on a single floor and the structure has been so designed that an additional storey can be added later if and when the necessity arises. The home has been planned on a simple and workable basis; the main entrance hall gives access to a well-lighted octagonal hall from which the main corridor runs down the centre of the building. Provision has been made for four single-bed wards, and seven double-bed wards; those wards opening on to the hospital grounds being fitted with French windows. In addition there are sisters' and nurses' bedrooms and a sisters' day-room.

Also included in the scheme is a kitchen for the preparation of the patients' meals, a reception room for the convenience of visitors, a recovery room for the use of patients who, after undergoing minor operations and not intending to remain, can recover before going home. There are also the usual bathrooms, sluice rooms and linen room.

The operating theatre has been designed as a complete unit. This comprises the operating theatre, the anaesthetic room, the sterilizing room and the surgeons' room, all of which inter-communicate with each other.

The exterior treatment of the building has been carried out in facing brick with the minimum of dressing, it being felt that a plain, restrained elevation would be most appropriate. Internally an atmosphere of quiet comfort has been aimed at for the wards. The floors, doors and furniture are in oak, the walls have been plastered with a special sound-deadening plaster and finished in a warm buff colour. The internal arrangements, the fittings and furnishings have been selected to impart a truly homely feeling to the home. The building is centrally heated throughout, all bedrooms have fitted washbasins and are wired for radio. A system of luminous signals has been installed. By this means patients can quietly summon the nurse and all noise and clanging of bells is eliminated. The building has been erected to the design of the architects Messrs Wadham and Son, Duke Street, Barrow.

End of an Era at the Alfs

The site of Kwiksave on Holker Street was a school for more than a century. Holker Street Schools, affectionately known as the Alfs, closed in 1988 as Alfred Barrow School moved to a single site on Duke Street. The school had started life on 10 January 1876. It had cost £11,000 to build and was designed by Henry Curzon. Just forty infants turned up for lessons on the first day but a month later that had grown to 158.

The school had been created as a local response to the 1870 Education Act whereby borough councils were required to set up school boards responsible for providing schools. The need in Barrow was obvious. In 1871 the town had 8,964 people aged under twenty years with just twelve registered schoolmasters. The Barrow School Board met for the first time in 1873 and decided that there were more than 3,000 children who qualified for school places. By 1877 the board had spent £40,000 on eight new schools for 5,000 children.

At Holker Street the school remained all-age until 1933 when it became the Hindpool Central School (Mixed). In 1935 it was known as Hindpool Central Boys'

The school at Latona Street, Vickerstown, shown in 1906. The building was opened in 1902.

School. In 1945 the name changed again to Holker County Modern School for Boys until they moved on to Victoria School in 1973.

Alfred Barrow Boys' School took over and in 1979 Holker Street and Duke Street buildings merged as the Alfred Barrow School.

Its most famous old boy was a First World War soldier, Lt William Thomas Forshaw, who was awarded the Victoria Cross. A total of twenty-nine of its old boys were to die in that conflict. Lt Forshaw, a former teacher, was called up by the Manchester Regiment when war broke out in August 1914. A year later he found himself in a vineyard in Gallipoli facing the Turkish army in a campaign which proved to be one of the war's greatest military disasters. The twenty-five-year-old repeatedly fought off swarms of attackers by hurling grenade after grenade at his enemies. He kept this up for a remarkable forty-one hours until he was relieved. He returned to his home town to a hero's welcome with gifts and a civic reception.

A Princess Comes to Town

Barrow has had more royal visits than most towns of its size, to dedicate new buildings and to launch many new classes of ships and submarines The first of these visits was in 1891 by Princess Louise and was seen as a matter of great pride by a town seeking to cement its place among the top-ranking industrial communities of the North West. The visit was reported in great detail by the Barrow Herald on 29 August 1891. St George's church needed money towards the building costs of new day schools and what better way to raise at least £500 than to have a grand bazaar with a real princess as star attraction?

The special train bringing the princess was 25 minutes late but she arrived to streets packed with thousands of spectators along the

The queen is crowned as part of Walney's Coronation Day celebrations for King George VI and Queen Elizabeth on 12 May 1937.

route to the Drill Hall. Duke Street had a banner across the road and banks and clubs had flags flying from windows. Cavendish Square was bordered with flowers and the Volunteer Band turned out to play the National Anthem The local newspapers could barely contain their enthusiasm for the big event.

The Royal visit to Barrow – Today is a red letter day in the annals of Barrow, this being the first occasion upon which it has had the honour of entertaining royalty. This will not fail in many instances to excite feelings of pardonable pride, and inexperienced though the town is in the manner of greeting it evidences the fact that it can rise to the emergency, though its populace are of such a cosmopolitan class, and proclaim its unbounded loyalty to the Queen and her family.

The announcement in the early part of the present year that the Princess Louise had definitely arranged a visit to the town was received with much satisfaction by all sections of the community, and there was a general fullness of confidence that suitable steps would be taken by the council – as expressive of the public wish – to invest the circumstance with that becoming dignity of recognition which all places invariably evince under similar conditions, and no solicitation was needed to cause members to put into practical effect the popular desire.

For several months the matter was allowed to lie in abeyance, but when the moment necessitating action arrived his worship the mayor brought the subject prominently to the front, and at a recent council meeting a committee was appointed to take into consideration what manner of reception should be accorded.

At subsequent deliberations it was recommended that a sum of £250 should be expended in giving a festive appearance to the streets, with a further proposition that an address of welcome should also be presented.

Zeppelin Passes over Barrow

One of the most memorable sights in Barrow for those old enough to remember it was the flight of the giant airship Hindenburg *across the town centre rooftops on two occasions during 1936. The* Barrow News *of 23 May described scenes of excitement in Dalton Road:*

Barrow had an unexpected visitor on Friday evening when the new German Zeppelin *Hindenburg* flew over the town on her return trip from America to Germany. The airship passed over Barrow at about 7.25 p.m. flying at a moderate speed. She was very low and her registration number and name could be clearly read by people in Dalton Road and over towards Greengate Street.

She was first sighted in this district from the vicinity of Bootle, coming from the direction of the Isle of Man and flying steadily towards the south. Her passage over the shopping centre of Barrow aroused the greatest interest and excitement. She appeared to be coming from the coast and steering a course that would take her across country. Every detail of her hull could be clearly made out and the deep note of her engines was the first intimation of her arrival. The swastika was clearly discernible on her rudder.

The airship made a return trip across Furness at the end of June. The Barrow News *of 4 July recorded its progress:*

As the Second World War loomed in Europe the Hindenburg *flew low over the rooftops of Lord Roberts Street in Barrow.*

Middlesbrough-born Barrow MP Charles Duncan. The former engineer was Barrow's first Labour member of Parliament.

The German airship *Hindenburg* passed over Barrow for the second time on Tuesday. She was flying fairly low and presented an imposing sight in the bright sunshine. On 22 May the *Hindenburg* first thrilled the people of Barrow when she paid a surprise visit in the evening about 7.30 on her return from America.

'The airship passed over Barrow on Tuesday in a north-westerly direction at 2.15 p.m. She then passed out over the Isle of Man on her way to America. Earlier in the afternoon the *Hindenburg* presented a magnificent spectacle to the residents of Grange and also many visitors who saw the big aerial monster cross the bay about 2 p.m., flying towards Barrow. She was also seen in many other parts of the Furness and Cumberland districts. She was sighted at Millom, coming from the direction of Barrow soon after 2.15 p.m. and passed over Bootle about a quarter of an hour later. The airship was then following the regular air service route along the Cumberland coast to the north. The Press Association states the *Hindenburg* was first sighted at sea six miles off Cromer at eleven o'clock flying in a north-westerly direction. The *Hindenburg* left Friedrichshaven for America earlier.

10,000 Came to See an MP

On 16 January 1906 a massive crowd of 10,000 people gathered outside Barrow Town Hall to hear the news that Charles Duncan was the new Member of Parliament for the town. Duncan, one of the first Labour MPs in the country, had beaten the sitting Conservative MP Charles Cayzer by a big majority. At 10 p.m. the result was flashed onto a lantern screen outside the town hall. Duncan had polled 5,167 votes against 3,395 for Cayzer. Duncan was carried shoulder high into the Engineers' Club. He had been sponsored by the Locomotive and Firemen's Union.

Hard Times in the Workhouse

The notion of cash benefits paid to those unfit to work or unable to get a job was frowned on back in 1902. The idea that you had to go into an institution and suffer for not being able to provide for yourself still firmly held sway. On 17 September 1902 Douglas Anderson, the medical officer, visited Barrow's workhouse at Roose. He saw men given the task of breaking stones all day or oakum-picking and living on a diet of bread, water and cheese. Dr Anderson calculated that the workhouse inmates were getting only half the amount of food needed to keep them alive.

He said: 'The whole of this wretched scheme starts with one fundamental error, namely: that all tramps are essentially idle, lazy vagabonds and that the only proper treatment to be meted out to them is starvation and punishment – cells, bread and water and stone or oakum – whereas, as a matter of fact, the majority of them are men out of employment.'

Among the inmates of Roose in 1902 were forty-one fitters, twenty-two blacksmiths, fifteen bricklayers, six charwomen, three clerks, three butchers, a watchmaker and two schoolchildren. Workhouse inmates who refused to do their work could be sent to prison for a month. They were only allowed out of the workhouse to look for work.

Calling Out the Fire Brigade

The growing town of Barrow had a fire brigade to call on in times of emergency from 1865. It started life in a cramped corner of the covered market and two converted shops in Hindpool Road. One of its biggest early duties was tackling a huge blaze at the Jute works in 1892.

Buttons and brass helmets shining as the Barrow firemen go on parade outside the new fire station in 1912.

Barrow's electricity used to be produced in Buccleuch Street, at the heart of the town's terraced streets.

A horse ambulance presented in 1900 by the Barrow friendly societies was also found a home with the fire brigade.

By 1910 the temporary fire station buildings in Duke Street were long overdue for replacement and in 1912 the new fire station opened on Abbey Road. At the formal opening the new motor fire engine was the star of the show. The new engine had been shown to the Barrow public on 11 November 1911 when it squirted a jet of water to the top of the Barrow Town Hall tower.

Bringing Power to the People

On 23 November 1929 Barrow's Buccleuch Street electricity plant was opened. Building a power station in the heart of a densely populated town centre would have planners in a frenzy today but in 1929 it was a matter of civic pride. The new plant had been built for Barrow Council by Vickers some thirty years after the first electricity generators had started to operate in Buccleuch Street.

At that time Barrow was not part of the National Grid and all the town's homes and industries were dependent on home-produced power. Many homes in the town were without power as it cost upwards of £10 to have a house wired. Electric lights were increasingly seen piercing the darkness on Barrow streets but gas lamps on side streets did not vanish until the 1960s.

At a mayor's luncheon to mark the opening of the new power plant, Alderman George Basterfield toasted 'the Electricity Undertaking'. The Electricity Department was the biggest money-spinner for Barrow Council and was based in new showrooms on Duke Street.

Preserving Law and Order

As a rapidly expanding Victorian town Barrow needed to expand the group which maintained law and order. Before 1881 the town had a small police out-station as part of the Lancashire County Constabulary – the nearest base being at Ulverston. On 1 May 1881 Captain Richard Nathaniel Cartwright Foll, formerly of the 32nd Light Infantry, was appointed chief constable of the newly incorporated Borough of Barrow-in-Furness. He was authorised to recruit and organize a police force of fifty officers, including two inspectors and six sergeants. The Barrow headquarters was in Cornwallis Street and plans were drawn up for a purpose-built station. Those plans were delayed by two world wars. Captain Foll was still listed as chief constable in 1898. His superintendent was J. Hartley and his inspectors were called Pritchard and Egan. It took until the 1950s before work got underway in Market Street to give Barrow a modern police station. On Wednesday 8 October 1958, the new police headquarters and magistrates' court was opened by the then Home Secretary and Lord Privy Seal R.A. Butler.

Trouble on the Streets

There is a tendency to look back on the 'good old days' as being a time of fine manners, neighbourliness and orderly behaviour. This was not always the case and high spirits could get out of hand. On 25 February 1920 the North-Western Daily Mail *reported on Hindpool being 'invaded' by trouble-makers.*

There have been nasty potentialities in a somewhat remarkable wave of excitement which has descended upon the Chatsworth Street quarter of Hindpool each evening this week. Both on Monday and again last evening, the neighbourhood has been invaded by bands of men, but the object of their incursion, and whence they came are, at least so far as the residents are concerned, purely matters of conjecture.

At least this much is known, that the men who singled the neighbourhood out for their attention on Monday were inclined to a disorderly tendency, and either by accident or maliciously the window in a house in Melbourne Street was broken; but no sooner had the occupant of the premises had a few words with them than the damage was paid for and the evening passed off without anything further untoward.

Last night more men went to the neighbourhood but simply sauntered about or leisurely gossiped in groups. A woman in Melbourne Street told a *Mail* reporter that from what she had heard among neighbours, these unusual features are a back-wash from the attack by a young Irishman on a police constable in Forshaw Street on Friday night. It was believed, rightly or wrongly, she said, that the associates of the officer's assailants live in the Chatsworth Street vicinity and that the men from other parts of the town were indignant at what had happened on

This arresting sight was captured on film in December 1923 as part of entertainment at Barrow Town Hall.

Friday night. She denied a rumour which was certainly current in the town this morning that matters had amounted in the district to a free fight and expressed the opinion that these freak incursions will cease.

Terror From the Skies

The Second World War was a new experience for Barrow – this time the whole community was in the front line. Night after night bombers brought terror from the skies as attempts were made to disrupt essential production at the shipyard and steelworks. No one could claim that the town was unprepared as the *Evening Mail* carried reports back in October 1939 of work underway on air-raid shelters and first-aid posts. The Barrow Blitz – principally in April and May 1941 – left 92 dead and 527 injured. A total of 618 houses were destroyed. Wartime censorship restricted what could be said in print about one of the biggest news events in the town's history. A typical report from the 1941 Barrow Blitz read: 'An enemy plane dropped a large number of incendiary bombs on a north-west coastal town this morning, causing damage to one or two shops and a number of dwelling houses.' The report hardly does justice to what it must have been like to live through.

Daily Drudge of War

Barrow's war was not just about bombing raids. There was the daily drudge of living with restrictions on the things you could do, the places you could go and the items available in the shops. War workers had

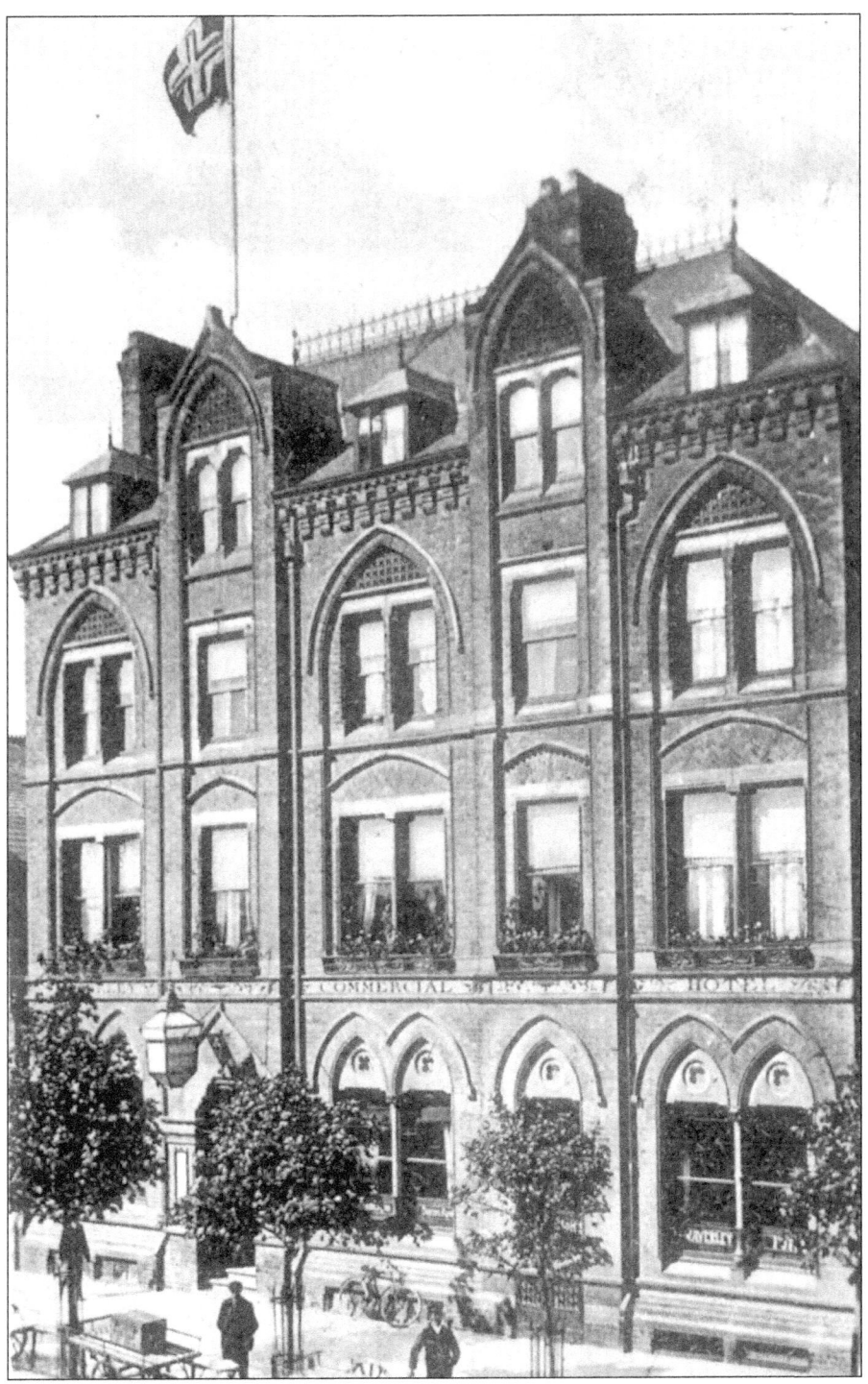

The Waverley Hotel was reduced to rubble by German bombs during the Second World War. This picture dates from 1913.

The Public Hall, which stood beside Barrow Town Hall on Cornwallis Street, was converted to a Civic Restaurant during the Second World War.

to be given priority on public transport so shoppers had to be home by 4 p.m. – or walk.

Rationing on fuel for private transport lasted well into the 1950s, as did rations on many other items – including sweets.

Celebrating VE Day

The news that Hitler's Germany had finally been defeated in Europe was greeted with jubilation in Barrow. Issues of the Evening Mail *during May 1945 were packed with stories describing how the communities of South Cumbria were marking Victory in Europe or VE Day. Many could not wait for the official events and got into a party mood as soon as the surrender order was issued to German troops. The* Evening Mail *reported:*

Flags and decorations appeared like magic and today's display was the best since Coronation days. The radio announcement last evening was the signal for rejoicing. Coloured lights went on in some streets and there was singing and dancing. There was another side to the announcement, however. It set a lot of people wondering whether they should go to work today and many did under the impression that the celebrations did not officially start until the Premier's statement. Hundreds returned home from the shipyard after a fleeting glimpse at the almost empty benches and deserted workshops. The works were closed today except for essential services. Schoolchildren uncertain of the position also turned up but quickly made for home again when a holiday was announced.

Tonight there are promises of bonfires unless the authorities intervene. Youths and children have prepared several at Walney and in other parts of the town.

Not all was rejoicing, however. Many a silent tear was shed for men who have given their lives in the cause of freedom and those who are still fighting the battle in the Far East were remembered. So too were the Barrovians killed in the Blitz just three years ago.

Planning for the Future

By the end of May Barrow was busy planning for the future – to replace buildings wrecked by bombs with new housing. An estate of 128 acres was planned at Risedale South. Work was due to start shortly and be complete within two years. The plans included a civic centre. Work was also expected to start within days on the 10-acre Tummerhill estate on Walney. This was to consist of 100 temporary bungalows. Barrow Borough Council gave a pledge to re-house at least 400 families by November 1945.

As Cold as it Gets

Barrow has suffered plenty of cold winters but the period from January to March in 1947 proved to be a record breaker – the coldest winter of the century. For three months the temperatures were regularly below 0°C at night and little better through the day. On the worst night the temperature dropped as low as –2°F or –19°C. The worst daytime reading was little better at 9°F or –12°C on 25 February.

The Holker Street stadium of Barrow AFC under snow in January 1940.

Ice, cold and frost had serious implications for the town. Electricity cuts left many homes cooking over an open fire with only candles for lighting. Coal was in short supply and navigating icy pavements brought thrills and spills in equal measure. On one frosty morning only ten of Roa Island's pupils arrived for morning lessons.

By 31 January there was no milk in Barrow as both collection from the farms and delivery to homes became impossible. By 3 February there were local newspaper reports of power cuts and many homes being without water due to frozen pipes. A day later coal went on the casualty list as the trains could not get supplies through to Barrow. By 10 February a total of 300 men were laid off, mostly at the paper mills, and Barrow suffered power cuts from 9 a.m. to midday and 2 p.m. to 4 p.m. On 14 February it was reported that 100 men were laid off at the David Caird foundry – now the Tesco supermarket site.

Barrow police resorted to sending patrols out wearing ice skates on 20 February. On 24 February a 100-year frost record was broken. Barrow had seen the longest period of continuous frost since 1841. The cold failed to stop the launch at Vickers of the ship *Accra*, although it took twenty-four braziers to keep the slipway free of ice. On 6 and 11 March storms and blizzards isolated Furness. The snow was too deep for the road ploughs to operate. As the weather thawed the inevitable floods followed from 19 to 21 March.

Barrow has suffered its fair share of harsh winters. This view from January 1909 shows deep snow covering the roofs and fields at Croslands Park.